a memoir by

Courtney A. Walsh

for Nana and Mara

Courtney A. Walsh
courtneyawalsh@gmail.com

Walsh, Courtney—Lipstick and Thongs in the Loony Bin
First Edition © 2007

ISBN: 978-0-6151-5953-9

'Diss'-claim-her

so that nobody gets it into their wee little heads to sue me, call me a big fat liar or otherwise discredit me in some mean-spirited way:

All of the people and events in this story are not in every case exactly the way they are/were in so-called 'real' life. This was done purposely to both protect the innocent (namely me) and because I have, on occasion, been accused of having the sometimes dicey combination of a vivid imagination with a selective memory. I have changed names and used initials in some cases to shield people's anonymity. Some conversations were recreated using a 'feeling' or tone of the situation...I do not generally go around with a Dictaphone recording conversations (though maybe I will start because some of the people in my life say some pretty funny things-- unintentionally most of the time) but I do have a good ear for dialogue and certain turns of phrase have stuck with me over the years. I did not mean to put the wrong words in people's mouths but to move the book towards its highest purpose. This is my story. It is a memoir. I can guarantee it is at least 96% (but I do not claim to be a math genius) accurate and serves a higher truth hopefully. That's the intention, anyway. That said, it is not fiction. It is not reality. It is truth. There is a difference. Truth is always personal, subjective and ultimately, when all is said and done and life is seen through a lens of love and humor...it is the best and only truth I know.

ACK! No-ledge-ments

(get down off that ledge—you're smearing the windowpanes)...

It would take a good portion of the rainforest to create all of the ink and paper needed to properly thank those who've taken this journey with me, but I will do my best because my first-grade teacher told me that's all any of us can do. Our best. My best wouldn't nearly be as good without the following people: For my family who've put up with more smartass behavior in one lifetime than any humans should ever have to endure. I love you all to the bottom of my baby toe, from the first baby tooth that fell out until the first grey hair that popped up...mine not yours. Kidding! Seriously, though, blessings to my little sister Kerry (and awesome bro-in-law Mike), my parents for reminding me daily that soul mate love is possible after 40 years together and still going strong as best friends and movie buddies—seriously—these two people alone keep Hollywood in business.

For all of my friends and adopted family along the way, Mama Dot—you are an angel in human form, Marilyn Howell and Mara Howell for reminding me that life is worth fighting for until the very last breath, to my friend Lisa Smith aka "Waaaackooooo" there is nobody I would rather go dumpster diving with for Burberry knockoff shoes at a Best Western than you, hon. To the AliBoyz and Galz: Leslie Lee, may your bent halo made out of crackpipes never tarnish, Deb Vaillancourt—keep quilting your dreams alive, Sean Casey you are my favorite Punkass Tinkboy, let the blushing begin! Duuuuude, sweeeeeettt. Steve Vinci, Mike Peach, Thad Krikorian, Gabe Cunningham, Ray Dechoretz and Orion Stewart for making life fun and interesting at a place that was neither fun nor interesting. For Mikey Noonan—Hey Mr. London McFancypants....when's our next roadtrip? Billy Holzman—so...free dental care for life, right cuz?

For Stephanie Checchi, Stacie Faria and Sherry Rose...you are each a little piece of divine yumminess and every time I am with you I laugh like I'm fifteen again. And speaking of yummy—for my gorgeous niece and nephew Sammy and Brady...Auntie CoCo loves ya bunches! Can't wait until you're both old enough to read. Joel Krikorian...you are fabulous, go on with yer bad self, boyfriend! To Danielle Chiotti and Andrea Mattei for convincing me there was a book here and who took me to lunch one fateful day three years ago to convince me that I was the one to write it. Thank you both for planting the seeds. To Don Snyder and Jesse Workman, thank you for my charmed Canadian Camelot time. Sue Hart, get your phone fixed, lady, eh? We have many phone chats to catch up on. "No-Nonsense" Nora Deschaine for the best apple pie and biggest grin ever. Paul Weinberg of Cabot Shores, the vision is unfolding. To Alyssa and Sasha—girls—FYM! JoNan Salisbury for sharing her "One Date" theory. Gratitude to Ann Martelle for your eleventh-hour editing help. Props to Carol Evon for your magic Reiki hands. For Stephanie Spaide, honey—don't forget your lipstick—you rock—and sweetiepie—the thong goes UNDER the control-top pantyhose to answer your question.

For Jess Bonome who does more than her share of heavy lifting in our friendship. Here's another book for your already overstuffed shelf, dearie. For my newer crew the 'Broth Babes', Jodi Gaess—Bette Midler wants her funny back! For Jacquelyn Ashley—Panini Queenie extraordinaire...keep laughing—the world needs your laughter. Meaghan Cronan—sweetie, we Irish lassies need to stick together, darling; Lori McDermott who originally coined the term 'Yippie' and Laura Patterson...life's there for you to make it whatever you want ladies—go for it! Linda Hogan, Leslie Arena, Christine O'Leary, Patt Gilmore and Linda Houle—you are all an incredible inspiration to me and I am truly grateful to know each and every one of you. Elianne Obadia—keep midwifing manuscripts!

To Dr. Larry—if I never hear the word 'spectrum' again it will be too soon but sincerest thanks for your steady kindness and your ability to help me relax into my life and let it unfold as it will. For the Ursuline homies, Jeannemarie Joyce, Beth Cronin-Bubar, Maureen Twombly, Gretchen Murphy, and the Randolph peeps, shout out to Amy Lam and Gayle Coughlin...If laughter were currency we'd all be bazillionaires by now.

For Robyn Patrick-Mayer and Stephanie Jennings...what a special gift it is to reconnect with soulsisters along the way, ladies~the Grid Kids are waiting... And a special thanks from the bottom of my heart to the top of my tiara to Dani Nordin of the zen kitchen in Watertown, MA (www.tzk-design.com), who designed a fabulous, splendiferously (What? It could be a word...) magnificent, gorgeous cover, who is also a web goddess extraordinaire and unrivaled graphic artist... it's finally happening!

****
*

"Approximately 20.9 million American adults, or about 9.5 percent of the U.S. population age 18 and older in a given year, have a mood disorder. The median age of onset for mood disorders is 30 years...women attempt suicide two to three times as often as men." ~ *NIMH (National Institute of Mental Health, 2006)*

Fore-(letter)-word

Sane is a four letter word. I wrote this book because I was tired. Most people when they are tired...take a nap. Not me. I have never gone for the simple solution. Ever. That's probably the source of most of my problems but that's a whole other book. What was I tired of? Thanks for asking. I was tired of the polarized images of so-called "crazy" people. I always think of terms like "crazy" and "sane" as though they have those invisible air quotes around them. If you get that concept then I think you will like this book. And if you don't, you might like it anyway...who knows? I am crazy...not psychic.

Anyway, I got tired of we so-called crazies being sorted neatly into one of two categories...Categories I like to call the "Creative, Misunderstood, Tortured Genius" and the "Village Idiot". If you just smirked, then you know what I am referring to...the ones who are artistically or scientifically somehow brilliant but cut off their own ears—or the ones who are somehow genetically challenged whom we unkindly envision sitting in proverbial corners drooling.

For most of us in the crazy club, we usually tend to live somewhere in between these stereotypical extremes. This book is dedicated to the tweeners...the ones who know that crazy isn't so black and white. That madness makes one neither special nor 'special' necessarily. There are those air quotes again. We tweeners know that our particular brand of crazy is neither a character defect, birth defect, (or gift depending on your perspective) nor is it something that sets us above or apart from others in a fragile ivory tower for emotionally sensitive (seen as both weak-minded and weak-willed) people in the clouds. But rather, that insanity manifests uniquely for all of us. And mostly, this book is written with unwavering love and empathy for those of us who manage in fits and starts to find the grace and beauty inside the crazy, and who feel grateful for the kindreds we draw into our lives along the way. This is dedicated with the deepest gratitude to the ones who walk us gently or drag us kicking and screaming through to the other side where true mental health lives and shines. Whether you are descending that downward spiral or recovering, stagnating or diligently chipping through ten-foot deep brick walls with a teaspoon...if you are the hand reaching for the drowning person you love or the one reaching for the life preserver...wherever you are on your crazy journey...this book's for you.

Thongtastic, darling

You may find this to be shocking news to hear from a woman in America in the early years of the new millennium, but I have never worn a thong. I could blame it on my weight or germ phobia or feminism or a dire fear of wedgies, but the truth is; I just never understood them. And it's ok, really. I met a woman at the hospital who would become one of those lifelong friends whereupon meeting you know on a gut level that you've known each other through lifetimes and there is that instant and total soul recognition before they ever even open their mouth. I'll call her Jacqueline. She was and is a paragon of 21st century glamour but with that wholesome girl-next-door twist. Jacqueline is six feet tall, looks like Carol Alt and has the unmitigated charm that gives her a star quality—mainly because of its endearing insecure undertones and sweetness to all she encounters. But she doesn't miss a trick--and she would become my confidante and co-conspirator in the battle against the brain in the months to come.

At 38 (yet looking at least ten years younger), Jackie's life had been parallel to mine in many ways...middle-class background, kind and loving (if sometimes clueless) old-fashioned parents, Catholic upbringing and overachiever tendencies. A few differences were that her father drank while my parents were virtual teetotalers--except for the occasional glass of wine (maybe two on holidays) with dinner twice a week at most. My father's drug of choice was his career as a highly successful educator. But our mothers may as well have been the same person...both beautiful and both married to successful men who were emotionally distant at times. In fact—my mother had even reigned in the mid-sixties as Miss Massachusetts which was an endless source of fascination for my sister and me growing up but a source of pleased embarrassment for our humble yet stunning mom. The story goes that my mother had accompanied her friend to a casting call for the pageant and was scouted from the audience to try out...the rest, as they say, was history and her biggest thrill was not getting her picture taken by the local paper in crown and sash but her first-ever plane trip down to Miami for the pageant itself. Her affair with fashion continued off and on for the next ten years while she did some runway and print work and even a gig as a hand model for a famous jewelry line. My sister and I were walking with books on our heads before we could read and wearing makeup before junior high.

Jackie's mother came from the same era more or less...the 'always look your best, even if you feel like crap' theory prevailing over all. She had once been on American Bandstand and closely resembled Annette Funicello while my mom was more the Natalie Wood type. About the third day after I had met my new pal in 'lockdown', her parents came to visit and drop off some clothes. Jackie's attempt had been much more 'serious' than most and had gone further than several others' on the ward. She'd overdosed and lay comatose for over 72 hours while her family was on tenterhooks wondering if she did revive, would she be irreversibly brain damaged? Miraculously, she came out of it ok and was brought to the hospital where I'd already settled in a week earlier. The red-rimmed eyes I'd suffered as a side effect of the carbon monoxide from my own failed attempt had faded to a less alarming pink, so that my eyelids no longer resembled those of an albino rabbit's. But Jackie's skin still held a bluish tint that even careful makeup couldn't camouflage. We made quite a ghoulish pair. After her parents left that first time, she was pawing through the stuff they'd brought her casually and came across a lacy thong spinning it around one finger asking me if her mother thought she'd be getting lucky? And in a smaller Ziploc bag were no fewer than 4 tubes of lipstick...all the better to look more schizophrenic with. We both 'cracked up' laughing. *Lipstick and thongs??!!* Later she'd ask her mother what on God's green earth she'd been thinking and her mother snapped irritably saying that she'd just grabbed things randomly and wasn't exactly thinking lucidly after her daughter's horrific dance with death thanks very much. Needless to say, she was not nearly as entertained as we were.

But I could definitely relate because my mother had packed me enough makeup to put on a Broadway show. (To be fair—I had asked for some foundation so I wouldn't feel like such a hag under the less-than-flattering fluorescent lighting.) What kinds of subtle (or not so subtle messages) were our progenitors sending us at this, the lowest moments of our lives? It was the old 'put on a happy face' and 'fake it 'til you make it' school of thought and Jackie and I were both appalled and amused by the all-too-familiar sentiments. It was incredibly telling how such an unconscious gesture could pack such an emotional wallop. We were 'pretty', dammit, and that was not something to ever forget or take for granted—even, apparently, in life- or-death circumstances. Knowing that our mothers meant well was beside the point. Feeling lost, misunderstood and self-pitying were still at the top of our to-do lists and being generous to those who had half driven us to suicide (as we romanticized, all the while knowing that they were not ultimately responsible—we were) was not a priority. Since suicide is the most hostile act one can commit against oneself—other than drunk-dialing exes at three in the morning crying of course, it stands to reason that all that self-hatred which had been turned inward for so long culminating in a death wish calling one to action must eventually switch gears and have another outlet—the Blame Game. There are some theories that proclaim that suicide is the highest form of 'screw you-itis'. There is definitely truth in that. However...the corpse is the one screwed the most in the end isn't it? A corpse can't dance, smell roses, kiss, or make love, let alone make amends can it? At least, none of the few I've seen anyway. So while the survivors of family members or friends are devastated, sometimes beyond repair...there is grief counseling and time to scab over wounds until one can successfully begin to function again. Time does nothing good for a corpse, and grief counseling is a bit late at that point.

Jacqueline and I would spend hours debating these fine points and other absurdities with each other and some of the other endearingly nutty misfits we became close with over the next several weeks.

We often talked about our biological clocks and how we felt resentful of our own ovaries' time restrictions.

"If I have to sit through one more baby or wedding shower I will shoot someone." Jackie and I shared this opinion that I expressed one day on a rant. I could tell from her emphatic eyebrow raise and sister-friend, sad-around-the-eyes smile that she got it. We both knew of course that I'd never *really* go Columbine but that on some primal level our friends were slowly and systematically murdering us with paper. We also knew that the sea of pink and blue ribbons or white and

silver wrapping paper, that were now all too familiar harbingers of the babynuptialhousebuying beast which would soon swallow yet another friend.

"Now, when these invitations come in the mail my heart literally stops for a split second. These people are killing me by degrees with their fancy paper and swirly fonts." Jackie would just laugh and nod her 'preaching to the choir' agreement.

Jackie understood all too well. Her attempt had followed a friend's announcement that she was preggers and it had been one of her final-straw moments. We felt as though our lives had slipped by us. We felt jaded and old. We felt our insides quite literally drying up. Society had told us we were old maids and therefore doomed to a spinsterdom filled with cardigans and cats. And I'm sorry—but as broken as we were.... neither of us was willing or ready to go that route...death seemed a welcome alternative when faced with unending loneliness, pitying glances from friends or worst of all, tiny, pretty napalm envelopes just sitting in our mailboxes waiting to explode our hearts and shatter our minds into irretrievable fragments...scattering pieces of our souls to the winds...carrying our disappointment and sorrow back to us again and again with written reminders and vellum inserts. It had all been so simple as children...we knew when we grew up that life would make sense.... we'd be safe from the wicked witches.... and all the promises of the early fairy tales of our youth would come to pass. We'd find our prince and our happily ever after. We'd ride off into stunning sunsets and decorate our castles with dream dust and butterfly wings.

We couldn't have been more wrong.

 Book One

The Blunder Years of Youth

The Little Match Girl

As a kid, my Nana would tell me stories of her travels, her childhood and fairy tales from the brothers Grimm and Hans Christian Andersen. These were pre-Disney stories. They were European fables with beautiful, sad endings and the basic philosophy that one should prepare children for the hardships ahead, not teach them to think of the fantastic but imbued with dark realism that *life is hard and at the end we all die*. Fables had morals and were to teach kids to fear shadows and to behave themselves or monsters would eat them...hence the evolution of the Boogey Man in the closet. Not cheerful stuff but important lessons were nevertheless imparted. That sometimes there was no happily ever after. Sometimes poverty could steal a little girl's life for no good reason. My favorite of these macabre tales was "The Little Match Girl". I'd beg her to tell and retell it...

Warm and tucked in with the weight and heat of her, enveloped in her cloud of perfume and her dangling gold chains and be-ringed fingers, my Nana knew how to set the scene and tell a story with all the trimmings. I was about six and she was babysitting me one night while my parents went to a holiday party at their friends' house. We'd had a New Year's 'party' of our own with ginger ale instead of champagne and peanut M&Ms for a 'treat'...everything was a party and there were always reasons to celebrate when Nana came over. But finally bedtime rolled around and it was time for a STORY.

"*Nana—tell it again.*" I practically commanded with the voice that only bossy children and drill sergeants can get away with...I wanted her to tell me my favorite story.

"Haven't you heard enough of that one? I've been telling you that same sad story for years and it never ends any differently. You know the little girl dies and you cry every time. I don't think your parents want me telling you that one anymore. You'll have bad

dreams. How about one of these books instead...you like Dr. Seuss...he's silly and fun."

"*Pllllllllleeeeeeeeeeeeeeeaaaaaaaaaaassssssseeeeee?*" I'd half-beg, half-whine--changing my tactic from demanding kid to panhandling indigent. I practically shook a cup with spare change in her face.

"*Ok...one more time, then but you help me because your Nana's getting old and I don't know if I remember it so well as I used to...*" she trailed off.

"*Nana...you're not old.... you're beautiful.*" I insisted.

"*And you're my special Courtney and I'll love you forever and even when I'm in heaven.*" She winked.

She punctuated this with a damp scratchy kiss...the kind that the wind brushed against. It would linger there a few moments before the breeze took it away and I knew that love was like wet sandpaper on your cheek. I knew it like I knew my own name which Nana had painstakingly taught me to spell a few years earlier...

"*When are you going to heaven?*" I asked.

"*Someday.*" Her bangles made that jingly noise I liked so much.

"*But not today, right?*" I implored.

"*No, honey, not today.*" she answered.

"*Good.*" Reassured, I settled back to hear the achingly sweet, sad tale of the Little Match Girl...

"*Once upon a time, there was a...*"she paused dramatically inclining her head to encourage me to join in; this was interactive storytelling, no passive audiences here. I had to work for it and it was like a game...

"*Poor, poor* (always double 'poor' for emphasis here) *little orphaned Match Girl!*" I chimed in proudly.

"*That's right...and she was SO poor...*" Head nod indicated it was my turn...

"*That she had no coat or sweater or even gloves to keep her little fingers warm. And she sold matches for a penny a box, right Nana?"*

"That's right my smart girl, she did...and what else...?" she stopped...

"And...um...I forget..." I shrugged.

"What time of year was it?" she urged...

"NEW YEAR'S EVE! LIKE TONIGHT!" I bellowed...

"Gold star for you!" she'd tease pressing her thumb to my forehead gently.

"And how many matches did she have left in the box?" she asked...

"THREE!" I squealed...

"Exactly.But did she have any food to eat?" she asked.

"No." I shook my head sadly.

"Did she have any parents to love her?" she prompted.

Another sad shake.

"So what happened when she struck the tinder to light the first match?" Nana cocked her head and I mirrored her curious pose.

"She saw a toasty warm fire. And she...ummm... warmed herself by the glow?" I half asked half answered.

"You really do remember this story, don't you?" I was pleased that my Nana seemed both proud and surprised.

"Yup." I smiled. *"I love this story, but especially when you tell it...you tell the next part Nana...what happened when she lit the* second *match?"* I wanted to hear the rhythms of her voice and to watch the expressions flit across her face like flipping TV channels fast.

"Well...when she lit the second match she saw a beautiful table with candles and roast goose (yuck I thought...who eats goose? But I kept quiet holding my breath as she went on describing the table laden with every kind of food imaginable)...

"...And there were all kinds of delicious goodies on the magnificent table and the little girl ate her belly full up with everything yummy and everything sweet."

"But **then**..." I said with a heavy, deep voice...I knew what was to come...

She resumed, *"Then the match went out and the table disappeared—POOF!"*

"Nana", I interrupted...

"Yes sweetheart?" jangle, jangle...

*"Did she get cold and hungry again when the fire went *poof *and then the table went poof, too?"* I worried...

"No, honey...she still felt warm and full." she conceded, to keep the story going and allay my six-year-old empathy. I breathed an exaggerated sigh of relief signaling for her to continue.

"Nana tell about the angel-grandmother now." I hurried her along with a yawn starting to get sleepy but not wanting to miss the best parts.

"When she struck the *third match* she saw a wonderful vision. Her grandmother from heaven appeared to her surrounded by a glorious shining light."

"Glorious shining light." I parroted in a tired whisper.

And as I drifted off she would lower her voice to a near whisper, too, and tell the saddest part of all...the part where the Little Match Girl was found cold and frozen to death the next morning on New Year's Day, her little stiff body curled up by her now empty box of matches. But she always wound up with the comforting nugget that she had reunited with her grandmother in heaven...in a place where she would never be hungry, cold or lonely again and where every night she slept safely and soundly in HER Nana's arms. The end.

With a big squeeze and a few more scratchy kisses she leaned over to turn off the light as I disappeared into a dream world of incandescent beauty--lulled by the echoes of jangling gold bangles and body warmth still left on the blanket...

String Theory

"Where do you think animals go when they die? Do they go to heaven like people?" My seven-year-old sister asked me soon after our cherished pet rabbit, Scruffy had just stopped being in the realm of the living one day. She lay on her stomach on her bed and I was sitting cross-legged on the pink shag carpet in our room reading a Judy Blume book.

"I dunno maybe there's a special animal heaven or a section in the people heaven for them or something." At eleven, older and wiser, I hazarded this guess, which seemed reasonable to K. but she still looked worried.

"What do **you** *think happens when you die?"* I asked, wondering why she still looked so confused. She clearly had a theory she was working out in her little head and I was curious.

"I know what happens." she asserted confidently.

"Really, how do you know?" I was intrigued.

"I just do." she shrugged.

"Well little Miss Know-it-All...care to share your thoughts with the rest of the class?" I needled, getting frustrated that she knew a secret and wasn't telling me.

"You mean you don't know?" she asked innocently and brattily all at the same time.

"Forget it...you're just making it up...you don't really know anything...you're just a baby." I huffed.

"I do SO know!" she sat up, peeved....*and "I'm not telling YOU!"* she wailed.

"Fine. I don't care anyway." I told her meeting her gaze.

We sat there staring each other down for a few beats and then I tsk-ed my disgust at her, shaking my head, rolling my eyes and picking up my book in one motion. Desperate that she was losing my attention, my older sister, reverse-psychology trick worked perfectly.

"Ok, ok...I'll tell you.... if you really want to know." she promised.

"OK...what happens?" I asked again.

"Well...first you're dead and then God wraps a silver string around you.... and pulls you up into heaven with the string." she pronounced very matter of fact.

I laughed scornfully. *A silver string?* This was her big secret? Her knowledge of the afterlife...people as puppets? Pul—eeze.

"What?" she looked deeply wounded... *"It's true!"* she wrapped her arms over her chest with lower lip thrust out.

"Ok smarty-pants...where does God wrap this string exactly?" I was determined to show her how silly her theory was.

She lifted up her whale turtleneck to reveal a patch of soft, pink belly beneath.

"From here." She pointed.

"From your BELLYBUTTON?!" I roared, cracking up...my baby sister had one BIG imagination...my giggles got louder and her protests more passionate...

"You don't know everything, you think you know everything but you DON'T!!" she screamed on the verge of tears.

I wiped my own mirthful tears away and saw that she was really upset.

"OK, ok...bellybutton, huh?" I repeated just to be sure.

"Yup. Bellybutton." Defiantly, she thrust her chin out daring me to laugh again.

I started towards her wagging my fingers menacingly.

"Is the string ticklish?" I threatened...

Her eyes widened... "DON'T" she pleaded.

I advanced and pounced and had her laughing and saying 'bellybutton' in two seconds flat. Her surrender was too easy so a second round of tickling ensued until she squealed for my mother...

"I'm TELLING!" she ran off to the kitchen...

"Mumma—Courtney keeps TICKLING me!" she tattled.

"TATTLETALE!" I yelled.

"Girls, behave. Go outside and play." Washing dishes, she had no patience for our daily sibling rivalries.

"K. tell Mumma about the string." I instigated suppressing a smirk.

"SHUT UP!" she warned.

"You know we don't say shut up in this house...K.... go to your room, Courtney, stop torturing your sister...you're old enough to know better." She scolded.

"Hey--I was just minding my own business reading my book and she kept bugging me. She's such a little pest! I wish I had my own room." I whined...

"I am not a pest. You're just mean!" K. Insisted.

"Enough, you two...K. go and think about what you said...you broke the rule and now you need to have some quiet time." (Being quiet and/or still were both terrible punishments for my hyperactive sister while they were blissful rewards to me)...

"Courtney, why don't you go over Amy's house and play or go ride your bike to Gretchen's?"

"OK"...I agreed, running out the door. I knew my mother was trying to make dinner and she preferred being alone in the kitchen without us "under her feet". I couldn't wait to share the silver string theory with my friend Amy, anyway. I knew we'd both howl at how bizarre it all was. Thinking that you became a marionette when you died seemed just too 'Pinocchio' for me. I figured heaven was a place where everything was fine and sunny, angels played harps and stuff and there was all the candy you could eat but never get a stomachache. My heaven made sense. The bellybutton thing was just stupid.

Later when my dad got home from work, tired, he unloosened his tie and seemed enchanted by K.'s recounting her string theory.

"*Yes—I think I know all about this invisible string...my little brother Herman told me about that when I was about your age.*" He stroked his chin as if remembering another time and place.

We knew all about my father's invisible little brother 'Herman'...whom he had repeatedly told us was actually little...like three inches tall. Herman was as familiar a comforting lie to us as the Easter Bunny, Tooth Fairy and Santa Claus.

It wasn't until many years later I would first read some esoteric teaching about something called an 'astral cord' (silver, in fact, I think) which supposedly anchors our soul to our bodies. Where does it connect? Well...right where the umbilical cord connects us in our mother's womb, apparently. When I first read that, I got chills all over remembering K.'s unflappable afterlife story.

From the mouths of babes sometimes stream beautiful truths that adults or even older children see as absurdities at worst and adorable at best...but usually just dismiss as the overactive imaginations of unformed minds.

As for me? I would never see a bellybutton in quite the same way again.

Spelling Bee

You didn't just win a man like my father. Everything came easily to him...he casually eased through life (but with a strong work ethic from a young age) like Robert Redford in 'The Natural' or as Hubble in 'The Way We Were.' Elegant in his three-piece Brooks Brothers suits (always tailored), hair sprayed and cologned, he was perpetually ready to take on the world. He'd risen from the teaching side of public education to the administrative side in just a few short years. At a relatively young age he was the Deputy Superintendent of a large inner city school system. He went from coaching and teaching and having summers off to meetings that lasted forever and took him away from us for longer and longer stretches. He looked the part. Gone were the sweater vests and corduroys and the era of suits and ties was ushered in.

My sister and I were never allowed to muss his perfect hair. If we tried playing beauty parlor with him he had little patience. One brush stroke and he'd rake his hand through his hair, smoothing it back in place saying, "Alright, that's enough." His was an innocent vanity of golden-boy habit, born in the spotlight and always needing to give off that air of impeccable confidence. He effortlessly maintained that illusion of ease, of sliding through life unharmed. My sister and I would watch him leave for work, the curtains pulled back from the front window, perching on our knees on the plush, blue sofa waving until our hands hurt. His return-from-the-office greeting was always the same enthusiastically screamed, *"DADDY'S HOME!!!"* He adored us and we adored him and most of all he adored being adored as any father would.

Canary legal pads with illegible scrawl always littered our house like forgotten banana peels. Discarded, crumpled yellow-lined paper balls filled our waste-baskets. We didn't know what this stuff was but we knew it was IMPORTANT. Mumma was beautiful and artistic and she kept the house shining and daddy was handsome, athletic and important. That was our whole suburban seventies childhood reality summed up in a neat bow.

"Do you have your list of words?" my Dad quizzed me distractedly one morning while putting on his crimson silk tie. He smelled like Irish Spring and shaving cream.

"Uh huh, I've been working on them with Ms. Baudette, too." I told him, watching as he made his mirror face...tongue pushing behind upper lip in deep concentration.

Ms. Baudette was the best third grade teacher in the world. I knew that because she took me for Chinese food as a 'treat' for being the first in the class to memorize and recite the entire poem called 'Owl and the Pussycat.'

"The Owl and Pussycat went to sea in a beautiful pea-green boat, they took some honey and plenty of money wrapped up in a five-pound note." I droned the whole poem in the singsong-y cadence that nine-year-olds find so comforting.

As Ms. Baudette handed me an egg roll she informed me that I was going to be participating in a Spelling Bee that would have schools from three towns in it and since I'd won the one for our school--Margaret L. Donovan Elementary, that I would get to be on a stage in front of a microphone and all of the parents and teachers would be cheering the kids on.

"If I win what do I get?" I slurped on my soda straw, *"Is there a prize or something?"* ever pragmatic, I wanted to know what I was getting into.

"Well...you might get your picture in the newspaper and a special plaque which is like a sign with your name on it...or maybe even a trophy if they have them...I'm not really sure." she admitted.

The night of the spelling bee my father went over the words with me again. My mother curled my hair with a curling iron and put it into barrettes with ribbons streaming down from the metal alligator clips. When I got up on the stage and looked into the bright light and saw the shadow people in the audience I felt completely calm and poised, ready to spell my little heart out. All of my earlier apprehension disappeared and it was just me and the light and the microphone and the words. Waves of words volleying. Say the word, spell it, repeat it. Wash. Rinse. Repeat. Rounds of elimination went by in a blur.

Finally it was down to me and one other boy. I missed the word 'handkerchief' with its sneaky silent 'd'. He missed one and then I got the next one and he missed the next one. The tennis match was winding down and it was my serve, my word, my moment and my win. I spelled the word 'through' correctly. The sentence they gave for usage had been "He looked through the window." My opponent had panicked and spelled it 'threw', throwing me the win. The applause was incredible and I must've grinned from ear to ear. I won something.... ME...and I beat a boy, too! I was now both pretty and smart not just for my Nana or my parents who had to love me, but also for the lights and the microphones and the strangers who were clapping. *For me.* My father pumped his fist in the air yelling *"YES!"* like he did at the TV sometimes when watching sporting events, only now it wasn't some guy in tights running down a field chasing a ball.... it was *me, me, me.* I got my plaque with my name already on it, which confused me. How did they know I would win? It never occurred to me that it was a certificate that they had made on a printer, one for each of the hopeful contestants that was easily assembled and put under glass like a picture frame with little brass screws to secure it into all of its mahogany glory.

It looked so official and important…did that mean I was official and important, now, too? Like dad in his suits with his yellow, lined legal pads? Could official and important people still play hopscotch at recess and slurp their sodas through a straw, I wondered?

My parents hugged me tightly and told me how proud they were. I was the 'best' they said…the absolute best. My father, already 6'4" grew to a seven-foot giant, swelled to the gills with the pride only a competitive athlete can appreciate when medals and certificates are at stake. I was his baby and his blue ribbon and so what if it wasn't sports? It was education, his turf—even better.

That night I was so wound up from the excitement and attention that I couldn't sleep. So many questions buzzed in my nine-year-old brain…. Having gotten a taste of this adulation I wanted more…. What could I win next? I mused…how would I top this? It gave me a stomachache and suddenly I wasn't sure I liked this important official business. It seemed like a lot of pressure for a little person. Was this how people in the Olympics felt after they won gold medals? This sense of fear and letdown and yearning for their next achievement but at the same time worried it might never come? My frame of reference was small. I didn't know much of winning except in relation to physical things…could you win other things besides good grades and spelling bees for being smart? My mom had won Miss Massachusetts and my dad had won lots of golf scholarships and tournaments but was spelling as cool as that? Well…. not as cool as the beauty queen stuff but definitely cooler than golf I decided. Everything seemed cooler than golf.

A few days later I saw it…. in black and white…a picture of the other finalists (losers) and me in my ribboned barrettes and curled hair receiving the almighty plaque. I felt strange yet happy to read my name underneath. It was reassuring somehow like my name matched the picture and one without the other would have been missing something. My friends thought it was 'so cool' and they said

I was 'famous'…I offered to sign autographs for them. Very generous of me I thought…. after all…that's what famous people did for their fans, right? But before I had a chance to get too Hollywood things returned to normal. The plaque on the wall became background noise like the strawberries in the wallpaper. No more existential angst about winning, no more stomachaches, no more lights or microphones. Just normal life…playing kickball until the streetlights came on, coming in for dinner, watching *Little House on the Prairie*, homework, tests, report cards….the usual. Every now and then, though, my dad would recount the story of the Bee and how tense it got towards the end when we were missing the harder words and tying things up, then tiebreaker then WIN! He always reenacted the way he flung his arms up in the air and yelled—*"Atta girl, Courtney, that's MY girl!"*

Atta girl. It may have been a spelling bee rather than math (which I frankly always sucked at) but this equation was simple. Winning equals important and special and lights and microphones and hugs and cheering and clapping and yes…even stomachaches. But stomachaches go away, pictures in the paper and plaques and memories last and linger long after the dust has gathered on them. Over the years I'd be reminded time and again that you didn't just win a man like my father…you had to keep winning him, his affection, his allegiance and his time were all doled out in glorious moments of golden shimmers…. fleeting and brilliant. It wasn't his fault he was attracted to winners. It was what he knew. He loved us for breathing but cherished us for winning.

Balancing Acts

My sister and I both loved the fact that our glamorous mother had modeled just like the ladies on the covers of the magazines at the grocery store. Her beauty queen status was magical to us. We wanted to know every detail about the time she became Miss Massachusetts and the many times she modeled beautiful clothes for fancy department stores.

"Mumma show us how to do the runway walk again!" was a popular cry in our house as little girls playing dress-up. Four years older than my sister, as a young preteen, ten or eleven at most, I had the hip swagger, turn, jacket draped over the shoulder, turn and glance over the other shoulder thing down and my smaller sister had the pucker and pout and jaunty head angles. Together the three of us cleared the coffee tables and created an invisible catwalk in our living room for our impromptu fashion shows. We were fabulous. We were gorgeous. We were MODELS.

Posture was heavily emphasized...

"Shoulders back girls, chins out, stand up straight, now move your hips like this..." She demonstrated the signature wiggle and sway that signals femininity across all cultures and generations. It was like playing fashion army with barked commands...clipped and no nonsense rapid-fire instructions until we would dissolve into giggles my mother laughing the hardest of us all.

"Here's a trick for balance that models use...each of you get a book off the shelf and watch me."

We all tried to stand as still as we could with the books so they wouldn't slip to the floor. It was a total exercise in exasperation for my sister and me. My mother's book stayed in place as she glided swanlike across the room. Thunk, thunk went our books and we wanted to stop the book balancing whining that it was too hard...on to the makeup!

"Here put a little color in your cheeks to bring out your eyes." We didn't know what bringing out our eyes meant...it sounded vaguely gross like our eyes might suddenly of their own accord pop out of their sockets or something...but mumma knew the makeup 'tricks'. Mumma knew all the model tricks because mumma knew everything about being pretty. With pink sponge curlers in our hair and flaming pink cheeks now came the Holy Grail of makeup time. LIPSTICK.

The way our mother revered lipstick and reapplied it several times a day was a ritual we were well acquainted with. There were no words needed to tell us why lipstick was very, very important...pretty much the most important part of the making-up process. We just intuitively knew it was an unspoken rule that pretty women always freshened their lipstick and had color in their cheeks.... (So did drag queens, schizophrenics, opera singers and clowns...but that knowledge came much later)...

"First, you purse your lips a little like this", she puckered into a kind of kissy face for us.

"Then you follow the lip line, like this..." she followed the lip line and we followed her, rapt and ready, eager for our turn up at lipstick bat.

"Then you smoosh your lips together and you're done!" Pucker, follow the lip line, smoosh, done.
Got it...

"Let me do it!" we'd each insist, swirling the lipstick up, but not too high, and gently laying the little top hat cap aside.

"Ok...but not too much...a little dab will do you. Don't waste it." she would caution.

"Wait until daddy comes home and sees us all pretty!" my sister jumped up and down in her excitement.

"Putting makeup on makes you feel good, doesn't it, girls?" We emphatically agreed looking at the altered versions of ourselves staring back from the mirror. Someday we'd grow up and be beautiful just like mumma. She had all the beauty tricks that the real fashion professionals didn't share with the ugly people. We felt really lucky to be in on the secret. We knew our mother was special and we loved her for it.

Later, after we'd had the chance to preen for our father who gave the obligatory wolf whistles of appreciation, the warm, wet washcloth came out to wipe our cheeks and lips. Our Shirley Temple curls got brushed out to keep the tangles at bay and we'd get into bed all clean and shiny and still pretty but not like before the washcloth. Now we were just regular again. Model time was over and little girl time had resumed. It was fun while it lasted and we knew we'd play again sometime...Maybe we'd grace the friends who were our best friends with some tricks we'd learned, showing them the secrets, too. Or maybe we'd just ride bikes instead and leave the lipstick aside for a while until we needed to feel pretty again.

Years later I'd remember these sessions with both fondness and wistfulness. Why did we place such a premium on looks? Why weren't we learning about how not to cringe when faced with the ugliness that life would inevitably hand us? It made me inexpressibly sad how we in my family (and the rest of the planet, too, it seemed) worshiped at the altar of all things beautiful, simultaneously learning that things that weren't pretty, well, they just somehow weren't as special. They didn't have that inner glow, that fingerprint of God. But, as always happens, when the pretty facades slipped and the ugliness crept in, I was unprepared for the imbalance of it all...my book kept slipping to the floor again and again with those thunks of disappointment and frustration. Because one thing my mother never taught us, one thing even she hadn't learned herself yet, really, was that the power of beauty is as fleeting as the moments that it shines until life's washcloth comes to wipe it away. The sun and dew illuminate a perfect morning glory at dawn yet that same flower could be wilted by nightfall, losing petals and leaves or dead a few days later. That morning glory (now losing glory) could be violently picked and stomped on by any passerby--just as any delicately featured face could be permanently scarred by a disfiguring accident, burned and spotted and cracked and lined by the sun or simply slackened by time's other mean ravages. Some things just can't be cured with a little color. Some illusions don't hold up in certain lighting. And sometimes pretty isn't just harmless fun...but an impossible dream to live up to.

Brushes and Crushes

In the fifth grade I had my first real crush. I didn't really count my younger years when I'd daydreamed longingly about Michael Mancini and his cocky class-clown antics or Butchie Drake who was always climbing trees and scraping knees. I was just a baby then…I was a big girl, almost in junior high now and Keith Karlson had arrived on the scene with all of his new boy allure. He was golden and his feathered hair was just like Shaun Cassidy's. His piercing ice-blue eyes set him apart from the other boys. Sitting behind him in class I liked the way his shoulder blades bracketed and as I traced the outline of them with my gaze, I imagined that was the exact spot where his angel wings had been clipped, leaving behind these stumps. It was the archetypal schoolgirl crush and I was the schoolgirl. He was the mini Adonis and all the girls swooned without knowing what swooning even meant.

On the day my mother was set to come to school and do a demonstration of Chinese brush painting, I woke up wondering if she would see my love for Keith Karlson as she stood in my classroom painting ancient letters on her rice paper tablet for us. Surely if she could read these slashes and squiggles she could read her daughter's love crime all over my face.

She yanked the brush through my hair. *"OUCH!"* I yelped. The bristles raked against my scalp and got caught in the snarling 'rat's nest' which had appeared overnight, somewhere between last night's bath and my morning Cheerios.

"Hold still, let me get the tangles." she said concentrating hard on her task, cupping one hand on the crown of my head while the other worked through the wild underbrush.

"That hurts!" I whined, as I did whenever she was being too rough because she was in a hurry to move efficiently onto whatever next household task awaited her. Dishes were driving her to distraction and we were both excited and nervous for her to come to my class.

In the car on the way to school, I nervously advised her, *"Mum, don't embarrass me or treat me different than the other kids, ok? For today just pretend I'm not your daughter and get up there and do your thing, ok?"* I pleaded nervously.

"Don't worry honey, I'll be good. I'm just not sure about this technique; this isn't like oil painting. It's a lot trickier to get the brush strokes right." She absently checked her reflection in the rearview mirror and ran her fingers through her hair flipping

it back out of her face a little. This half head toss was as much a part of her as breathing and as familiar to me as her perfume.

I knew she wasn't listening, "MUM, I'M SERIOUS!" I barked....Keith Karlson could *not* see me as some kid whose mother painted weird Chinese letters and stuff. He had to see me as the fabulous creature I wanted to be but wasn't. He had to see *my* angel wing scars and heavenly glow, too. I worried she'd ruin my chances as the future Mrs. Karlson.

"Alright, relax, you're making me more nervous. This isn't easy you know, getting up in front of a bunch of strangers. Your father's the teacher in the family, not me." she revealed.

The houses whizzed by and typical scenes of morning in the suburbs were evident everywhere...people getting the paper in their robes, men in suits getting in cars, kids with backpacks and lunchboxes waited for the bus.

"Mum, they're not strangers they're my friends." Well...most of them were, anyway. Ever since Ronnie Borley had called me 'fat cheeks' puffing his own out to make his cronies split their sides laughing a few years earlier he'd become a mortal enemy and I wasn't overly fond of Kristin Banes' bullying ways, either. *"Walsh—YOU'RE DEAD!"* screamed across the playground field one afternoon had given me nightmares for weeks.... But the rest of them were pretty ok.

"And anyway," I continued as I helped her unload the blocks of paper and box of brushes and inks, *"they're fifth graders, it's not like any of them are exactly Chinese painting experts."* I rolled my eyes, my new signature move. Eleven and already the smartass.

"Alright, Missy...let's go in." we both steeled ourselves to face the 25 little art critics eagerly awaiting us in my homeroom. I was arriving with the celebrity of the hour and it gave me a flutter of excitement. My stomach did a little lurching dance with my throat, which had suddenly tightened with the anticipation of seeing KK and my mom in the same room. My universe was getting tinier by the minute.

As my mom set up her easel the teacher introduced her and the seat squirming got stiller, voices hushed to whispers then were silent as she took out her brushes, explaining...

"These are different than regular paintbrushes which are made out of wood and horse hair or sometimes even boar hair," she continued, "these brushes are much lighter, they're hollow like straws and they are made from an Oriental plant called bamboo." A giggle rippled through the room as someone in the back, (probably stupid Ronnie Borley), hollered *"A rigibamboo!"*

The teacher tsked loudly at him and filled my mom in... *"It's from a line of a song they all know."* She spoke in shorthand female grownup to my mother who'd looked confused and nervous for a minute, having thought the kids were laughing at her demonstration. My mother visibly relaxed then and resumed her instructions on how to hold the brush. Looking around me I saw that everyone was holding their yellow No. 2 pencils in the exact delicate way that my mother was holding her bamboo brush and they were all dipping their pencils into invisible inkwells, carefully mimicking her graceful movements.

And I noticed something else, then, too. Keith Karlson had his chin in his hand and was staring intently at my mother, not at her painting, or her brushes or the rice paper block on the easel. And I looked around to see that some of the other boys were in this same staring pose looking dazed like they were moonstruck or had taken Love Potion Number Nine. *Disaster! Keith Karlson loved my mother!* In fact, ALL of the boys seemed to love my mother. They were definitely not looking at her like she was a mom. They were seeing the model, the beauty queen, the movie star. My mother looked over at me then and gave me a little wink. The next day when I got to school the kids huddled around me telling me how 'awesome' and 'cool' my mom was. I held my breath and waited to hear what Keith would say. And finally he chimed in...

"Your mother's so pretty, what happened to you?" he asked with a serious expression. The other boys snickered. *"Shut up!"* I thought to myself. In my own mind I prepared a defense, *"Everyone in my family says I look just like her...they even call me 'little Barbara' sometimes."* I would announce proudly. But I got very quiet and just looked back across my desk into those baby blues that every girl wanted to do the backstroke in...I couldn't summon any smart responses and my eyes

wouldn't do their new casual, heavenward roll. *Nothing. Zip. Zilch. Nada.* The silence stretched between us and opened up a Great Divide of time stopped, almost moving backwards as it hung there full of his question and my sudden muteness. After what seemed like an eternity, KK just shrugged his shoulders, which no longer seemed like the place where wings had been attached, and he turned away. Staring at the back of his head, I noticed a really big tangle in his Shaun Cassidy mane and thought to myself, *"Boys shouldn't have hair long enough to tangle into gnarly rat's nests."* And I felt an overwhelming sensation of panicked failure, of never measuring up. I wanted to brush his hair, to paint for him, for him to really see me. I was overtaken by the sensation of a book sliding off my own perfectly brushed, untangled hair, the weight of it sliding invisibly to the shifting ground below me.

Turn that Frown Upside Down

"You were looking for an orchid and I will always be a dandelion. You were looking for a tealight, and I will always be a forest fire. I am the 4th of July. You could go blind in my light. I am the Northern Lights, I am invisible. I am a dandelion, I am forever wild." ~ Antje Duvekot, Pantjebare Publishing, ASCAP

Years after I had long recovered from the realization that I was never going to be Mrs. Karlson, my friends and I walked into the gym at the Xaverian Brothers High School for the school dance...We all gave each other that *"Here we go."* look. The look that soldiers must give each other from foxholes right before they lob grenades at the enemy. Or firemen before entering a burning building. That unspoken agreement to conquer. Our grenades were our lip-glossed, Giorgio-scented selves. Heading into the gym, the wave of Polo cologne and boy-sweat fought with ivory soap and mouthwash. The Polo/boy-sweat mixture inevitably won out. It was, after all, a gym--and decades of athletic events were permeated into the very bleachers...Who knew wood could hold smells so viciously? As a Catholic who'd grown up in New England—I knew that church pews might absorb a faint, musty, incense-y smell that had that slight familiar whiff of holiness and mothballs. But this was no church smell...this was a soup of hormones and industrial cleaners. It was a smell that said—*"Enter at your own risk."*

We loved that smell and feared it all at the same time. We couldn't have articulated any of this at fifteen but it was evident in our nervous fidgeting, our obsessive hair smoothing, our beelining as a group (safety in numbers) to the girls' bathroom to primp when we started to wilt. The SMELL followed us...the boys, however...they stayed on their side of the room across the Great Invisible Divide. None of us were adept in the ways that students who attended co-ed nondenominational (public) school kids could easily interact or well...*speak* to each other.... this Great Invisible Divide was a buffer and a barrier to our hormonally-addled, private-school brains. So we danced in groups...again that safety in numbers thing....We vogued like Madonna, we woke up before someone go-goed to Wham, and we alternately yelled and whispered, kicking our heels up to SHOUT *heyeeeeeeeeeeeheeyyeeeeeeah.*

And then.... if we were very lucky.... or very unlucky.... we would climb the Stairway to Heaven. The world's longest song when stuck with a sweaty-palmed boy that wasn't of your choosing....or blissful, furtive making out (as much as one could get away with before getting tapped on the shoulder by the Catholic kissing police) with your crush of the hour. Ironic to be avoiding getting felt up to Led Zeppelin by Brother Burke's stern tap on the shoulder. Thrilling and odd...that combo of shame and desire, nervousness and comfort of the warm body you were leaning into or in most cases away from to avoid choking on the bottle of cologne that particular boy had chosen to BATHE in before venturing forth for the evening to the very place he'd been shooting hoops with his friends earlier...Maybe even on the very spot you were swaying right now while trying to politely hold your breath and smile as though you were thinking dreamy, romantic thoughts and not wishing for the end of the night when you could hug your pretty, but disappointed friends goodbye and get into your dad's car for the ride home to your pillow. We all went in hopeful and came out disappointed.... this was the standard pattern. All of my friends were these unassumingly beautiful, sweet, fun girls. We never really got asked to dance—whether because we were too shy or the boys were, we could never really figure that part out. We just knew that rejection smelled like cheap cologne and boy sweat. We tried our hardest to pretend we didn't care. Occasionally one of us would be lifted from the sad vibe of desperation into a cute guy's waiting arms...but these experiences were few and fleeting. Mostly we had ourselves and, of course, each other as consolation if we didn't get asked to dance or worse—if we did the asking and were refused. We knew that we weren't our mothers, we weren't husband seekers...but we yearned for affection and to feel wanted, chosen, pretty.

One night after one such crossing the Great Divide to ask a boy to dance only to be devastatingly refused in front of his posse of pals' experience, I felt horribly depressed by it all. My dad saw my downtrodden face and started in asking a few innocent (yet loaded) questions.

"How'd it go...? Did you have fun with your friends?" he broached the subject gingerly knowing that unexploded grenades and teenage girls were tense territory.

"I don't want to talk about it!" I barked and abruptly started sobbing, emptying myself of the Great Invisible Divide that had suddenly invaded my broken pubescent spirit. *"Nobody ever asks me to dance!"* I wailed...Untrue, but exaggeration is the cornerstone of teenage female dramas and I was not immune to its siren-song charms.

"What's wrong with me?" I begged his older, wiser male insight.

Looking at my red, puffy, tear-stained face I'm sure my father was stricken with the panic that only fathers of teenaged daughters can know intimately. The fear of saying the WRONG thing...and the knowledge that there is no RIGHT thing.

"Maybe you just need to smile at the boys more?" he thought out loud.

"SMILE MORE???!!! Dad—my cheeks HURT from smiling." I retorted with a disgusted sigh. I turned and watched the other cars and houses whiz by in a saline soaked blur. Silence followed, punctuated by the soft tones of talk radio....some sports game no doubt and my occasional sad sniffles. If your heart broke—did it dissolve in your chest, become some form of snot and then ooze out of your face, I wondered? Because I had liquefied heartsnot everywhere and not a tissue in sight. I was literally slimy with sorrow.

"Check the glove compartment for some napkins…there might be some in there." My dad suggested helpfully. I was fifteen, and a total mess. Mascara everywhere—I looked like a bad Spanish soap actress. A few straggly snot-filled napkins later we pulled into the driveway of our suburban home and all I wanted was the cool cotton pillow against my hot, sticky cheek. Well—first I wanted to wash my face and de-slimefy it…with ANYTHING but ivory soap, and then slip into my pajamas and into bed. I wanted to sleep for the next five years and wake up to have all this teenager business behind me. I wanted a father who didn't tell me that the way to a boy's heart was through false smiles across a Great Invisible Divide…. hoping that someone might see the sad girl behind the smiles, under the shiny lip gloss and love her anyway. I wanted the sweet smell of victory of swaying in someone's arms who smelled like heaven had opened up and put him there, boy sweat, cheap cologne, nervousness and all…for me. Just me. But instead, I had a disintegrating wad of wet drive-thru napkins, a raccoon face and a vow. To never, ever go back to that gym again—not smiling, sobbing or otherwise. I was drained of all hope of romance ever taking me into its warm embrace and I was so stuffed up with heartsnot that I couldn't smell a thing.

Dangling

My feet are dangling in the water of my best friend's pool. There is that oily slick of dead bugs and leaves swirling on the surface and I'm mesmerized by the play of light and shadow and by the circular movement of my feet in the water. I don't feel connected to the feet or the bugs or the leaves…yet somehow I am at the center of it all…though my mind hovers and takes in these details with numbed detachment. The breeze gently ripples the trees making that *shhhhh* sound…a librarian's stern warning translated through a sudden summer wind. It's late summer and my best friend's father has recently hanged himself—causing us all to stop and wonder at this lonely death in a shitty, dark basement, surrounded by empty beer cans and a lifetime of disappointment, a stark contrast to these gorgeous, sky-blue summer days.

At the funeral, my friend seemed old. So much older than her nineteen years. Sorrow had quite literally aged her overnight so that she appeared more like a hunched over grieving Italian war widow than the bubbly cheerleader I'd known for years...Her brother—a few years older was clearly in shock...his strength born of that nameless New England stoicism, bore her up as they received waves of relatives they had met once or in some cases, never. Their mother had died of cancer at a young age. They were now young adult orphans, facing the world at large with the defiance of those who survive a family member's ultimate shame. *Suicide.* The word never spoken, except in hushed whispers at the edges of the cloying-scented, flower-filled room.... the smell of shame, the pall of it...settled over the room like an itchy wool blanket and over all of our lives briefly with it's relentless accusations.

All the usual cliches were tossed about...selfish...weak-willed...martyr....victim...I swished these thoughts around in my head as my feet did their egg-beater dance in the water, banging occasionally against the concrete edge, hopefully hard enough to leave a bruise—or to at least bring me back to myself, my body and its physical solidness. It's aliveness.... not dead like the leaves or the bugs or my hair or a myriad of other dead things.

His corpse was bloated and the coroner's makeup barely hid the rope burn on his neck. One of my friends had the macabre need to share with us that my friend's father would've soiled himself—hanging was an ugly business. We just glared at his insensitivity and tried erasing that image from our fear-soaked thoughts. Letting go of life voluntarily and the indignity of your bowels letting go involuntarily was too much to comprehend. Too much.

A dragonfly lay on its side on the water's surface, struggling with a broken wing...some predator had ripped the silken transparency, rendering its owner disabled, and drowning as it struggled. I tried scooping it up with both hands cupped around it to give it that buffer of water between those delicate, damaged wings and my unintentionally clumsy hands. I poured the dragonfly onto the concrete and watched it die a slow, painful death...all the while seeing the metaphor for the suicide that none of us could've prevented...no matter how gently we cupped our hands around my friend's wing-injured dad...he was lost the minute he hit the water. Sorrow's oily slick had snared him and now—he, like the dragonfly, was gone.

My feet dangled and stopped their figure-eight motion. I envisioned another set of dangling feet…I couldn't avoid that image no matter how hard I tried. We all dangled between life and death daily. Our feet barely touching earth, we would go through the next few weeks just trying not to drown with him…it was like he was pulling us from somewhere just beyond visibility, into that world just beyond pain.

Soon autumn would come and the pool's navy nylon cover would be pulled over it just as his eyelids were closed gently for the last time by a stranger's hands. It seemed bizarre and frightening and surreal and awful. Yet it was his choice and we all knew that. It was his choice. Whether he had chosen wisely—we all knew that wasn't the question and that there could be no other answer but 'no'. He had chosen recklessly and thoughtlessly. Without care and definitely without love. On that we were all agreed. So why did I envy his quieted dangling feet and the dragonfly's final wing-flutter? Why did I want to switch places with a corpse and stop my own inner swirling? These questions terrified me so much I had to cut them off at their own knees. I couldn't allow them to dangle…I couldn't allow them to beat their dying wings against my teenage fears of immortality. I just couldn't let them in. So I slammed the door on these thoughts, locked the key and swallowed it.

A few years later my Nana would be the one in the box…the funeral was held on a snowy, grey winter day and the ground was frozen solid. I remember thinking that my fiery grandmother could probably melt the earth—even after death. Her hands had always been hot, not warm—hot. She never had a circulation problem like other women her age. She used to joke that if hell were air-conditioned she'd happily go there—winking…besides she'd probably be in good company. Her hot, papery-smooth, dry hands always warmed my always-freezing ones. Her lips were permanently chapped as long as I knew her—no matter how many times she reapplied lipstick or Chap Stick. It was like she was burning up from the inside…like all that life force was a furnace of sorts. I couldn't wrap my brain around the fact that I'd never feel those hot hands holding mine or scratchy cheek kisses ever again. Lots of people lose a grandparent and it's sad...a rite of passage. When I lost mine it was like I was being gutted with the sharpest knife ever. I knew she'd want to be remembered not mourned. I knew she wouldn't approve of my lingering grief. But I was lost. The intensity was like that of the five-year-old who loses her mother's hand in a crowd and panics that they'll never be reunited again, but that she will she drift off into an alternate, unsafe world of strangers. It was heartbreaking and soul-wrenching and it was the worst pain I've ever experienced. I still sometimes feel as though chunks of my heart were amputated that day. The phantom pain comes and goes, usually worse at holidays, mostly. So it's no wonder that I had a picture of her with me in the car that fateful 'garage' day. To me...I was going 'home' and she was the only real home I'd ever felt. I imagine that she might get annoyed with me now and tell me I'm being overly sentimental and maudlin. She would certainly want me to find a new 'hero' (her word for boyfriend)...but she was the only hero (besides my parents later and my brave friend when she was fighting colon cancer) I could revere. Because she was also deliciously imperfect and real. She had a capacity to love that was astounding and inspiring. And she was also just funny as hell. She was more the type of grandma to tell the odd slightly naughty joke than to bake cookies. Her brand of love was much more daring and unique. She'd say, *"Let's have a party!"* which could be anything from eating peanut M&Ms on the couch while watching Wapner or dancing wildly to her old records. One time she made me toast with marshmallow fluff, a hot dog and I washed it all down with cream soda, potato chips and Whitman's chocolates. I puked for a day and a half but her effort was appreciated—it was an interesting meal—a creative but failed experiment to be sure. Her unfailing encouragement and *"Atta girl!"* attitude bred in me self-confidence and the soul of an adventurer. And now, whenever I get itchy feet to travel somewhere new... she tickles them with a feather from an invisible boa urging me on. Someday we will have that reunion, and we'll have a lot of catching up to do. I'll tell her all about my travels and about the boys I've flirted with along the way. We'll have a party all right. But *not yet*, she whispers. Not yet. I swallowed some more...lump in throat, bulging like an ugly goiter, but I swallowed the grief down like a thirsty baby at her mother's breast. The problem, as any pediatrician can tell the parent of any toddler...with swallowed things…is that they always find a way out. It may take a long time for them to work their way through your system. But they will always come out, seeking the light of day, waiting for the tiniest ripple of a breeze to dare them to be silent.

Book Two

Are we there yet?

Ironically, as I'm sure you have figured out by now, despite its glamorous and cutesy title this isn't just a pretty, little fun story. You may be feeling like I've pulled a bait and switch on you...I prefer to think of it as the 'spoonful of sugar' approach. But perhaps it was a calculated trickery—packaging this as a fluffy beach book and then making my reader *think*. As a lifelong reader myself—I know that I personally hate to *think* when I go to the beach. In fact—it's the last thing I want to do—I want mindless entertainment to complement the pounding surf, squealing kids building sandcastles, competing radios and seagulls squawking as they fight over French fry remnants in those little red and white, gingham-patterned boat containers.

Just so we're clear...there's no formulaic happy Hollywood-esque ending, nobody will ride into the sunset with swelling violins. Because let's face it—in real life the heroine usually just has to wake up and do laundry and last night's dishes the next day after the whole riding off into the sunset thing anyway, right?

So consider yourself warned...better late than never, right?

While the rest of this book does deal with mental illness, it is not, however, an exaggerated tale of what it means to be 'crazy'. No straitjackets...only the 'Quiet Room' and frozen oranges. It's not 'Girl, Interrupted' or 'One Flew Over the Cuckoo's Nest'. Now that I've told you what it's NOT and shared a bunch of sweet, sad, funny and relatable (hopefully) tales to lure you into the weird world that lives in my head...the rest of this book is a story of the stigma that still surrounds mental illness even in this new millennium. But not in a preachy/obnoxious/protesting/whiny/strident sort of way.... Frankly, I don't have the energy for that kind of writing, nor has it ever appealed to me as a reader. It is more a personal story and guide map about not being conquered by life's little moments as they add up over years and decades. And it's definitely an ongoing, ever-evolving plan of how to rebuild hope one millimeter at a time. It's my version of your story.

But, ultimately it is MY story and yours is different. Your story might begin in a classroom, or at your boyfriend's house, or at the grocery store. But mine really begins in an enclosed garage with an engine running. Everything I gave you, dear reader, up until this point was simply back story for context. So if you want to—please keep on reading...and while I hope you will slog on through the labyrinth that is my grey matter, I will not be offended (because really how will I even know?) if you choose to throw this book at your cat in exasperation (poor kitty) and instead peruse a magazine article on fifty ways to wax yourself hairless with household items. I hear Elmer's and masking tape is quite a fun combo! But you will consider yourself warned and I will consider you brave to plunge ahead (again...not that I will really know either way but you get the idea) . Here comes the suicide part....Let's all take a deep breath together...

So—the garage. I was 32-year old able-bodied, attractive (or so I'd been told), kind, charming woman who had simply had enough of this world, this life and most of all--of herself. I was ready to permanently retire from planet Earth, but somehow through the grace/graze of a beebee gunshot wound to my mother's left knee, an unnaturally abbreviated trip to the emergency room and my dad's nine iron, I lived to tell about it.

I had no tangible reason to be so desperate. My vanilla upbringing (with its bland traumas aside) had been a perfectly 'normal' (whatever that means) middle-class childhood complete with parochial school, braces and crushes on boys. So how did I end up listening to Sarah Maclachlan's 'Angel' grasping a picture of my dead grandparents when I was found trying to poison myself with carbon monoxide? The picture was a black and white shot of them waving--probably snapped on one of their many trips to Atlantic City. In this particular photo they seemed almost beckoning. Both had a twinkle in their eye and it almost felt like they were keeping me company while I waited to fall asleep for what I'd hoped would be the last time. The damned Grim Reaper must've been out sick that day because he clearly had other plans. Well they do say only the GOOD die young, right?

Under my girl-next-door smile was a screaming, tormented harpy being pushed further and further toward oblivion. On the day of the attempt, I had reached such a place of unbearable psychic pain...months of insomnia, years of uncontrollable mood swings, and decades of not feeling like I ever fit in... anywhere. Despite the brilliant facade I consistently acted out for the benefit of my friends and family, things under the surface were anything but 'fine'. By the time I actually got around to the actual attempt, to me, there was nothing extraordinary about attempting to end the nightmare.. It was the most natural thing in the world. In my distorted mind, all I could think of was that I was finally going 'home'.

I'd been living back with my parents for a few months when one day things came to a last-straw, camelback-breaking crescendo through no real fault of any of the key players. It was a day that started like any other with a beautiful, sunny dawn and ended with screaming and sirens...Grown children and parents nearing retirement is an awkward pairing at best and deeply humiliating for all involved at worst. My parents and I had a longstanding relationship of misunderstood love wrapped in fear with the best of intentions all around. Basically your garden variety family stuff with some drama thrown in from time to time...we were, after all, mismatched temperaments from the start. My first full sentence as a child had been "Gimme the orange".... No 'please' just GIMME. And from that moment forward I think they became afraid of my voracity for life and mistook it as greed or bad manners—my highly emotional responses were chalked up to lack of tact and drama queenery. My enthusiasm was always met with cautious optimism or guarded skepticism. "Be careful" was a popular family mantra.

For a long time, (well just the first thirty years of life really but who's counting?) I resented their negative interpretation of my personality...them labeling me 'difficult' only made me determined to be more so if since I was going to be called a drama queen, or brat then what was the point of following the boring parental advice to "behave, be nice, be pretty, be smart"...It was a recipe for disaster and it was well meant...but it was just too friggin' hard. Impossible really...I often accused them of wanting a china doll and not a daughter. Once you've been cast in a role within the family, the cast ultimately reaches a stage where it itches to the point of insanity. (As it turned out—quite literally in my case). One day you wake up and realize the cast, the role no longer fits, there is no broken soul fragment endlessly healing under crackling plaster. There is no weighty bone under puckering skin. *There never was.* Only then can you cast off the cast, the role you can't remember signing up to play, the plaster dust and the heaviness of the illusion of it all—the *you* that never was; the reflection of flaws and fears of the other people on the stage with you dissolves like threads of the most fragile chrysalis, and the wings inside begin to dry and unfurl. Then, when the memory of one's pre-formed self begins to fade, all notions of wrongness, rightness, goodness or darkness, meld into a quickening, a marching toward what that unnamed longing has been yearning for. This opening forward and releasing backward gives us the aerodynamic lift to experience the wind for the first time, from beneath our feet, beneath the earth, propelling us in an upward spiraling swirling dance of unending possibilities. I would like to claim these as my carbon monoxide-soaked thoughts. But they were merely ideals I'd known in some part all along. And tried to articulate in clumsy ways over the years to friends and family members. They must've just thought I was stoned or something.

My parents, needless to say, were thrilled I was so verbal at such a young age *"She's a genius!—honey say the alphabet backwards again"*. Together we went from winning the spelling bee one minute to diatribes on premarital sex and Catholicism the next *"She's a bitch with no soul!—you're grounded...FOREVER!"*. It must have seemed like the blink of an eye to them. But you really can't go home again as many of the post-college twenty and thirtysomethings I know have reminded ourselves when in financial crisis, between jobs or going through divorces, breakdowns, etc. New England real estate being what it was and my having been a gypsy for over a decade, I had no savings to speak of and minimal debt, but minimal earnings. When I moved back in I was not in a great space, literally or figuratively. In fact, NASA would not want to explore this frightening abyss frontier of misery. Not with all of the shmancy shuttles and dried up food we could provide them with. *"No thanks...think I'd rather stick a flaming hot iron in my eyeball...all set."*

On New Year's Eve day, about three weeks after my baby sister's wedding, the holidays coming and going, and my decline sliding further and faster than anyone, (including me) realized, my mother, father and I decided to go for a walk and enjoy the rare winter afternoon sunshine. My mother went off on her own and my dad and I were walking and talking. Which fairly rapidly turned into walking and fighting and a lecture about getting a 'plan' for my life and not leeching off of him forever, etc. I was in my early thirties now and needed to become more self-sufficient. He was completely right—while I'd had long stretches of financial stability, I'd also had bouts with bailouts needing help to always 'get back on my feet' and this time—I was still horizontal and my feet weren't even near the floor, let alone standing on them. He'd been supportive, he'd been patient...he was getting antsy.

Even though I knew everything he was saying was true, even the deeply painful *"You can't just leech off me forever,"* comment, I didn't need to hear these sentiments echoed outside my head since the same thoughts had been haunting me and giving me insomnia for months.

As I listened to his dadlike, pep talk expressions, *"You've got to get a plan."* sounded to me like, *"You are a total loser and I want my overachiever daughter back."* I was getting 'F's on his report card. On my own report card I was giving myself "Zs" and not the restful kind. I felt like I had to invent a whole new alphabet to accurately describe the depths of loserdom I had plummeted to...A to Z didn't cut it...no gold stars here...not even lumps of coal...just nothingness. *'IsuckIsuckIsuckIsuck'* was the mantra in my head getting louder and louder with each passing second.

I started freaking out on him defensively saying *"I KNOW Dad, don't you think I KNOW all of this?!"* with such agitation that if I could've peeled my skin and hair off in that moment I would have done it if just for the distraction. Things were escalating when my mother hobbled over to us interrupting the flow of the argument to announce that she'd just been stung by a bee and her knee was really bothering her.

"A bee?" I asked....thinking that was odd in New England in January. She just glared at me as if I were the 'bee' and wordlessly told me to *'shut the hell up and stop irritating me and your father'*. She'd mastered these withering telepathic glances over years of practice with two bratty, back-talking female teenagers. We all silently piled into the car and rode home in the kind of quiet that screams with recrimination, disgust and despair. *Yousuckyousuckyousuckyousuck*.

When we got back to the house, she confessed that it wasn't a bee-sting after all but rather a random 'Beebe' gun shooting perpetrated by a car-full of rowdy teenagers. At first I thought it was the most bizarre (and slightly funny, actually—like the suburban version of a drive-by) thing I'd ever heard. Apparently, she hadn't wanted to add fuel to my or my father's rising tempers so she'd made up the bee-sting story to distract us. My shame was complete. I might as well have shot the Beebe gun myself. Here I was an ungrateful, difficult daughter whose own mother was afraid of her reactions and felt the need to tiptoe around them. It was the final push…I had just come through my younger sister's picture perfect wedding, followed by the holidays from hell, and I had no fake smiles or game face moves left. *Thissucksthissucksthissucks.*

It had been a whirlwind season of the kind of exhausting havoc that only weddings and holidays can create, complete with seemingly endless trips to malls. Sterile and antiseptic places where I had to find all the resolve I could muster not to burst into sobs at catching sight of myself in store window reflections. The hag staring back had bags under her eyes; she was wearing shapeless clothes and had stringy unwashed hair. Who was this stranger? This black hole of suckage who just pulled everyone in around her with sad, yawning eyes that seemed to have that perpetually watery thing that allergy sufferers and alcoholics are so famous for. Who the hell invited this bloated, pimply, pale creature that had kidnapped me and hijacked my body? She had appeared sometime during the wedding rehearsals, gift-wrapping, the endless gifts and STUFF that all had weight but no meaning. It seemed she was a permanent, annoying houseguest who had far outstayed her welcome. The piped-in Christmas music and wedding march became loathsome. Suddenly Pachelbel was now my sworn enemy and 'Jingle Bells' scratched nails on the chalkboard of my spine. This stranger was getting stronger and I was rapidly disappearing and giving her the remote control to my life.

Deflated, demoralized, horrified, exhausted and yet numb all at the same time. It was New Year's Day and I was done. Do not pass go; do not collect two hundred dollars total bankruptcy kind of DONE. No resolutions except one...don't be here this time next year. Or tomorrow for that matter. *Lifesuckslifesuckslifesuck-slifesucks.*

My parents headed off to the emergency room, conveniently leaving a vacant space open in the two-car garage. Our little late afternoon stroll to catch the dying winter light was becoming a deadly disaster of seemingly epic proportions. Depression distorts thinking and mania sharpens resolve...woe to the unlucky girl whose pendulum is hovering dead in the middle (pun intended) wildly swinging back and forth so rapidly that she can't keep up. I feared things would only get worse for all of us and was convinced I was so worthless and such a burden, one that my parents would never get out from under as long as I was under their roof and in their lives. So the sickest, yet eerily, calmest, part of myself decided that it was time to free us all and I silently thanked the Beebe bullet that had serendipitously shot this opportunity into my life...my death. Beebe, bee-sting, behave, be nice, be sweet, be quiet, be a good girl, be careful, be gone.

The flip side of depression is supposedly unexpressed anger...And I was definitely angry...so very, very angry. Pissed at how my life had turned out despite all of its early advantages and promise, angry at always feeling like nothing I ever did or said was good enough for me or anyone else (but mostly for me). I was supremely bullshit at the universe and even irrationally angry at the damned Beebe...which I was quickly coming to see as the symbol of both my damnation and redemption--all in one small piece of twisted metal lodged into the bone of the person whose bones had once lodged me. It was a cold rage that burned itself out in a flash and then I was in a sensory-heightened, yet emotionally removed, state--body and brain battling...suddenly I had a garage and at least a two or three hour wait in the emergency room to work with and I certainly had a motive. Time, method, murder weapon and detachment collided and I pulled my car from the driveway into the empty slot...closed the garage door behind me and got in, turned the key, tuned the radio to my favorite station, because really, who wants to end a crappy life with crappy music? That's no fun.

And I waited. Waited for sweet sleep, sweeter release, and the sweetest final song that would take me away like Calgon bubbles to my Nana's waiting embrace. Ok, it's not like I thought she'd be waiting in heaven with a tray of cookies or anything. First of all, any recovering Catholic worth their pillar of salt knows that hell is for suicides but I figured that was a technicality I'd deal with later. Besides, Nana had never been the baking type anyway, which had been one of my favorite things about her. She was a rebel, a feisty redhead way ahead of her time and I felt the one and only person who had ever really gotten me. Her scratchy kisses from always-dry sandpaper lips were more soothing than abrasive. Her travel tales and cheerleader ways... the word 'can't' was not in her vocabulary. There were a thousand tiny things about her that I remember...Her creativity at getting you to do things you didn't want to was not merely bribery but beauty. A nickel a cup to get juice down when sick was her deal. Dixie cups of liquid consumed transmuted and became money and checkmarks on a chart. She invented positive reinforcement long before any psychology book articulated it as a viable childrearing technique. To her, I was a wonderful, magnificent creature to be cherished, praised and adored. This was not spoiling, for children are not fruit that can rot from within unless we do that to them with our own needs and expectations. This was LOVE. At Christmastime, her love came carefully wrapped in tiny packages, perfect sizes for little fingers. Trial size shampoo and hotel soaps were imbued with fairy magic. Maybe that's when I missed her most—the holidays lost their festivity and sparkle when she died. For years I'd missed feeling small and safe, sitting under the dining room table amidst an ocean of adult feet and shoes and socks and cooking smells until someone would cross the border into kid-dom and lift the tablecloth inviting me back to their world. Nana always had me sit next to her. I was hers and she was mine and nobody better dare come between us. It was known. I missed her like I missed my own heart. She was home to me. So in my haze I had hoped that some sort of reunion would be possible. I desperately wanted, no, *needed* to go home.

These hopes were dashed (smashed really) when I, just starting to drift off, heard my parents' screaming and panicked voices. *"Attention-seeking little bitch!"* is the phrase that will haunt me until I do actually kick it. Then there was the *"No! No! Oh God! Call 911!"* fanfare and I stubbornly wouldn't open the car door, half-conscious and half holding onto whatever fumes I could. Not willing to give up the dream, or in this case nightmare, yet. My father used his nine iron to smash open the windows and drag me out while my mother called the ambulance. And off to the emergency room, for the second time that day, we all went, they in their car and me escorted by Mr. Eager EMT who kept trying to fasten an oxygen mask to my face even though I kept firmly pushing his hand away. He finally gave up, perhaps figuring that there was enough oxygen in the air and I was obviously at this point more than semi-conscious. I believe he probably noted some scribble or other like *"uncooperative little shithead narcissistic girl with no real problems in life refused oxygen mask"* on his little official clipboard. It was a long, surprisingly quiet ride to the hospital. No chitchat, no small talk, thank God for small favors on that one, and no squawking walkie-talkies. Just the wailing siren barely drowning out my own inner screaming. Happy frickin' New Year.

Really? They still do that?

In the ambulance the unbearable shame set in...which was more toxic than any poison I could've imagined or ingested. That was one thing I'd come to learn at the hospital—most failed suicides feel this sense of overwhelming shame—not merely that they'd tried to kill themselves—but that they hadn't succeeded to 'even get that right'. I sat through group after group of people talking about the guilt of having hurt their families. I remember when my sister first called me after having found out...she said: *"How could you leave us with that legacy?"* I didn't know how to answer. I clearly couldn't answer. Because my thoughts weren't about legacy...they were consumed by death. Death hammered me all day long with seductive ways to get out of the hospital to try again—this time would work and there'd be no room for error. But finally after months of dealing with the 'so-called' professionals (who willingly admitted that medicating is a hit-or-miss game and nobody knows why something works or doesn't work) and more tweaking of meds, things would finally begin to lift a bit. But I didn't know this yet. I didn't know that after trying on and discarding diagnoses from the DSMIV (the psychiatric Bible, Koran, Torah and Satanic passages all rolled into one) they would find a label for me, and it would stick to me for the rest of my pitiful life...or at least I could get out of the rat hole and try again

Before the attempt, for about fifteen years, I'd been on every pharmaceutical concoction available with little to no results that lasted any significant period of time. Therefore, at the hospital I was told I made an excellent candidate for ECT (electroshock therapy). Excellent candidate for zaps to the brain? Well, wasn't I the lucky one? Who even knew they still did such a thing? Wasn't it archaic? Medieval even? After a very hard sell and blur of paperwork I was signed up for a course of ECT, (12-14 treatments 3x a week for several weeks) told not to eat or drink anything after midnight the night before a treatment and that I'd be anesthetized, wake up a little headachy, might experience some jaw discomfort (that turned out to be the understatement of the millennium—I frequently felt as though I'd just gone ten rounds with Mike Tyson) might have short-term memory loss but the payoff was that I would probably see rapid results in the mood improvement department. I succumbed to the pressure I felt the doctors were putting on me to give ECT a chance.

One doctor in particular had a hangdog face that I remember more than his words. His face held more sorrow than anyone I'd ever seen...even the fellow tortured binmates looked downright chipper compared to this man. I started not knowing where my pain ended and his began and as I watched his mouth moving and listened to his bizarre explanation of what ECT really was exactly. I floated in and out catching only snippets of what he was saying. I felt like I was underwater and his words bubbled to the surface of my consciousness in little bursts of oxygen...

"...juggle your brain chemicals".... "Tremendous success with this procedure", "...not like it used to be", "not like in the movies,"...I think he thought his words were soothing and reassuring. I was having a hard time following the thread. All I kept thinking was... "I am a statistic to this man, not a human being." It was both chilling and comforting. If I was a statistic then I was a blank slate...he didn't know my history other than what was on the page in front of him, he didn't know

my Nana--she wasn't on his clipboard. He didn't know my sister or what she looked like in her wedding gown, that wasn't in my medical chart. So to him... electrically charging my grey matter was merely a 'procedure' while to me, it was a Stephen King film.

Dr. Bassett Hound was just one in a parade of people who came to talk to me about ECT. They grimly reminded me of the alternatives (there weren't any) and played the guilt card to the hilt...asking me if I wanted to continue to put myself and my family through this agony? Subtle. They insisted that it was far more humane nowadays, I'd be put under anesthesia and *'wouldn't feel a thing'* and it would give me a boost to get me *'back on track'*. Clearly my brain chemistry was betraying me—but would punishing it help? I was unconvinced but too tired to put up a fight anymore.

During my second week on the ward after the 'brain juggling' paperwork was all filled out, I was ushered into a brightly-lit operating room where there was a young doctor who looked like a sleek character from a soap opera flashing his bleach-toothed grin at me. He assured me they were going to *'take good care of me'* which I'm sure was meant to be comforting but instead totally creeped me out. The anesthesiologist administered the IV and an icy cold burn seeped through my reluctant veins. Let it be said here that this was a last, last resort—ok actually—the suicide attempt itself had been the last resort and anything after that was done out of total numbness and exhaustion. The previous five years or so I had become a Reiki practitioner (ancient hands-on healing art), I had drunk fish oil by the gallon, bought a light box for S.A.D (seasonal affectual disorder—since my mood problems and insomnia worsened in the winter months), tried exercising regularly, and I even cut out sugar and caffeine for periods at a time until I decided that life without chocolate was depressing in and of itself. I was also in talk therapy, had tried every drug that Eli Lilly offered—twice—to no avail and wrote regularly in a journal to attempt to make sense of the madness that gripped my life squeezing ever tighter as time wore on. However, after 7 ECT treatments and lots of short-term memory loss (which did return later as promised) I stopped the zap fest and went back on the medication merry-go-round. I made this decision one day when I asked a friend I had known for ten years how we had originally met…it was at that moment I knew that this wasn't working for me. If I was going to forget the important details that linked me to my life then how would that help me recover?

When I first got to the 'bin' as I affectionately referred to it to friends—trying to be colorful and put everyone at ease that at least I hadn't lost my sense of humor…it was determined that perhaps I was 'med-resistant'. Since I'd been on antidepressants at the time of the attempt this was a safe-bet assumption. After five hours of interviews during which I started to wonder if I was actually being accused of some crime I may have forgotten that I'd committed…like high treason in my sleep or something…I was admitted to be committed. Voluntarily. What they fail to mention about this process is that it is easy to sign yourself in, not so much to sign yourself out. Rather like a sinister version of the roach motel except instead of killing you they were doing everything in their power to prevent you from killing yourself.

At some point early on, I realized that I wanted to at least get well enough to regain basic freedoms if nothing else. To never again have to suffer the annoyingly gung-ho MHS (Mental Health Specialist) wake me and my fellow binmates from our zombie sleep with his insipid— *"Time to get up now…c'mon, c'mon let's go people…"* As though we were kids who would be late for homeroom. Or to have to endure the humiliation of being herded like cattle on our evening walk. Or the ultimate indignity of having someone watch me shave my legs and then returning the razor until my privileges were at a level where I could safely have 'sharps and flames'. We all shared the same lighter on the smoke breaks ostensibly so some pyro wouldn't get cute and try self-immolation by Bic or something. I wanted my life back, such as it was. I wanted out. My sister's wedding had been one of the things that had pushed me over the edge of sanity into a darker place where death seemed the natural antidote to chiffon and champagne toasts, to yards of white and pearls and lace embroidered hearts…each of which had eaten chunks of my spirit until I looked like a Pac Man ghost rife with holes and getting ever more and more transparent.

And now I was for all intents and purposes imprisoned for my grand gesture, my so-called cry for help had gotten me the best help my insurance could buy while my sister got back from her honeymoon to settle into her life as a newlywed I was trying not to become a part of the Newly Dead brigade.

On the ward, I sat in the tight, stuffy phone booth one night after dinner and before lights out and listened to her lecture me with a tight voice about my selfish actions. I envisioned her Tiffany bracelets and the flash of her diamond ring on her perfectly manicured fingers, my own fingernails bitten nearly to the quick, raggedy and bloody in contrast. I could practically see her unpacking her honeymoon suitcases in her condo as I traced the pen marks carved deeply into the wood beneath the accordion silver phone cord stroking it absently and thinking of our other silver cord connection, The graffiti captured it best...some previous inmate had scrawled "There's no place like home."

"*I love you very much...I'm glad you're ok.*" She signaled the end of the conversation and her words hung awkwardly for a few silent seconds stretching between the years and miles between us.

'Til Death Do Us Part'

As we were growing up in the seventies and eighties, my sister and I were and are, even now, night and day. She being day and me being night, of course. She, the sunny cheerleader type—me: the somewhat morose, yet still oddly charming and quirky deep thinker. She played with Barbies and me—I wrote stories, poems, created little plays with friends and scoffed at the blonde vapidity and plastic pink world that I at an early age had figured was never to be my destiny. K. is four years younger and light years away in personality as I'm sure you've gathered from my description thus far. But, to be fair to both of us—these were early roles that were cast and there were lots of exceptions and crossovers in our personality traits over the years but you know what it's like when you are seen in a certain way—temperament can be determined by the subtlest of moments and is reflected back to you by your parents' joy or disappointments, their attention or lack thereof. When she was born I thought I had a living doll to play with and love and kiss and hold. As soon as she could walk she'd run away from my smothering attentions and even a six-year-old knows when they are not wanted. She became a tomboy and I was a bookworm, she became a follower and I was a leader—both academically and with a small crowd of friends a few of whom I maintain friendships with to this day. I was the teacher's pet while she struggled academically. All those years she was more than a few steps behind but she caught up and surpassed me in the beauty department, in the luck department, in the romance department and in the baby-making department.

While I'd never really been a jealous person—suddenly when K. became engaged I felt a profound sense of stabbing envy unlike anything I'd ever experienced. It took the wind out of me and consistently surprised me with its overwhelming intensity during the year I went through the maid of honor motions doing my obligatory duty all the while dying a little inside with each bow-filled event. I knew it was unbelievably selfish, and immature and ridiculous even. Yet it seemed like someone had taken a highlighter to my life and underlined all the recent failures and all the early promise I'd shown and was mockingly demonstrating how they just didn't add up. While I was licking my wounds and trying for the millionth time to get back on my feet again—recently fired from a crappy retail job, she was planning a new life with my soon to be brother-in-law...The last date I'd had had gone so poorly the convent started looking like Club Med.

Somewhere in between cake tasting, dress shopping and the bridesmaids' weekend in Newport, I became sadder and more desperate with each pre-wedding event. I can't blame all of my unhappiness on the wedding—it merely represented something for me—a turning point or milestone I feared I'd missed. I knew that all of the Barbie time she'd logged which I'd so casually scorned had paid off in some way. She was headed for a family life that I had desperately avoided yet at the same time yearned for on a cellular level. While I traveled and globe-hopped, she had built the foundation for a lasting love with my wonderful brother-in-law. Handsome, solid and completely devoted to K. he sees the world as a place that is better with her in it and that shines through his eyes each time he looks at her. His adoration for her is unhidden, naked for all to see and as strong ten years into their relationship as the day he first asked her to share an ice cream cone with him on the quad after approaching her in their college library. He is inherently good. He would do anything for his family. He is not a boy though he is fun and playfully boyish at times, he is a 'man' like the old Jimmy Stewart and Cary Grant types, there's an easy elegance and grace about him tempered with jocky masculinity. He's Abercrombie and Fitch meets old Hollywood. The words 'husband' and 'father' were stamped on his birth passport as though those roles were destinations he was bound for someday. He and my sister are one of those perfect couples that are the envy of all around them. In their aura of love and sweetness suddenly, having danced in a red dress on a ledge in a nightclub in Spain or lain topless on a black sand beach in Greece seemed like great stories but nothing deeply meaningful or fulfilling. Oh, yes—I was sending out the invites to the pity party and it was to be quite a bash.

Apples and oranges is a dangerous game as I've learned over the last few years. About 4 or 5 months after their gorgeous wedding and picture-perfect honeymoon my sister and her husband became pregnant. Worried that I'd backslide into a black hole, I unraveled the messy feelings about my natural biological clock and Noah's Ark wish to pair up and procreate. I worked through this with my therapist who assured me that I wasn't going to hell for not being overjoyed at becoming an aunt rather than a mother. And he even hinted that I might come around in time—he was right. I knew it the minute I heard my unborn niece's name. It was petty and silly and stupid and normal to feel these twangs again... but I was tired of wasting energy on things that hadn't worked in my life, dubious career moves, rocky relationships and all my seemingly failed attempts to reinvent myself into a kinder, gentler and skinnier me. I'd like to say these were the lessons I learned during my time in the bin...but mostly I learned how much I hated having my freedom constricted and that I wasn't good at being confined. And that there aren't enough Oreos, pills or cigarettes in the world sometimes. It's a short trip for some to the place inside where your heart and mind crack at exactly the same moment, but for most people it's a meandering path, it takes years of swallowing who you are and takes a long while to recover. So while my sister nursed her hurt, angry, superior and self-righteous thoughts about my selfishness and family 'legacy', still basking in the glow of taking her vows and snuggled safely in her condo in Connecticut with her Labrador, handsome state trooper husband and spotless SUV—I fought the battle of a lifetime in a far less glamorous setting. Bitter--party of one? I'm nuts remember? Doesn't mean I don't love her completely or that I wouldn't walk through fire for her but I get to be bitter for brief passing moments while I work on rooting out the craziness...

Perhaps it was karmic payback for all the years she felt I'd let her down as a big sister. I tried to understand—my mother claimed she'd stepped in telling K. not to visit because she didn't want her to see me 'this way'. 'Til Death Do Us Part' meant different things to us now. Since we'd never really been particularly close, her absence wasn't a shock but it was disappointing. I understood her anger and need to disconnect. I even understood her needing to see me as a drama queen trying to get attention. What I didn't understand was how Barbie had driven such a wedge between us so early on. Though Barbie is a scapegoat, I know. The truth is...we were born into a suburban family entwined by blood—a soup of DNA linked us but we may as well have been born during different centuries, cultures and on different planets for all the similarities between us. However, for all the complexity of the gaps in our natures I will cherish her until death do us part—and let's hope that's not anytime soon. Doesn't mean I don't still think she's a pain in the ass sometimes or that she still doesn't occasionally wish she were an only child when we are together on holidays and the claws come out. But hey—that's love—it's not a greeting card...but most of the time it's pretty ok...even when it drives you beyond the limits of yourself and back again. And that's the true legacy I hope I can leave behind. But most days I don't think in terms of legacy but in terms of what it really means to love while we are still here. What love will I leave behind? What stories will people remember about me the most? And how will I keep myself from sliding into that hole again? For one thing...I'd probably avoid weddings for awhile.

 Book Three

Beginnings, Endings and Saggy Middles

Getting Married Gangsta Style

When my Barbie lovin', multiple Tiffany bracelet-wearin', Coach purse carryin' little sister told me she was planning on having a Hummer limo for the bridal party to travel from the church to the reception hall I almost sprayed Diet Coke through my nose with a shocked snort-laugh.

"I'm not sure I have enough bling to qualify me for a spot in your rap-mobile." I teased.

"No—it'll be great—we'll all fit in together—the groomsmen and the bridesmaids and we'll have a blast." she insisted...and I just stood there squinting and picturing her with a gold tooth sparkling under her shiny M.A.C. lip-gloss.

The day of the wedding we all gratefully piled our taffeta and tuxedo-clad selves into the nightclub with wheels since it was blizzarding out and 6 inches of snow were expected to coat New England, decorating the world white for K.'s special day. This was a practical foresight that I hadn't credited my trendy sister with... an all-terrain, all-weather vehicle that cruised through a half a foot of snow like it was nuthin'..."*'Zat the best ya got? Pffftt....gimme more!*" the sturdy car seemed to sneer. Inside, the row of lights along the truck's ceiling made it seem like an airplane runway in reverse. This thing was built to PARTAY...heeeeeyyyyyyy.... say what, what...we were suburban gangstas rollin' up in style and they better not mess with us, yo, or we'd lawnmower their asses. Old school style—the kind you *push* not ride motherblanker!

I'd made it down the aisle, through the 'I do's' and now there were four hours or so (and counting) until the entire previous year of *"Your sister's getting married and you're a loser with no boyfriend, job, or apartment of her own nanananananaboo-boo"* was winding down...grinding to a merciful halt at the Pines Pavilion...a lovely, generic site that was home to many a wedding...not sure how many previous guests had rolled up Fifty Cent style but here we were. And there would be alcohol. Lots of it. I knew I didn't want to get drunk...but I welcomed the kind of gentle buzz that would take the edge off of the pitying looks from my aunts and help me get through the thousands of frozen smile pictures that awaited me at the Pines Pavilion. Talk about a mental institution name if I'd ever heard one...a premonition? Preview of coming attractions?

What makes it a pavilion? I wondered as we walked in the unimpressive front door...It just seemed like a slightly larger Elks Club from the outside—granted it overlooked a lake (frozen) and there was a gazebo out back (rapidly disappearing under snow) but overall—it wasn't impressive as a building itself. It was only as we entered Winter Wedding Wonder/Fairyland that I realized that brides didn't care about the outside of this place. It was the inside that caught their attention. Room after room of pink and green and cream-colored decorations that put English gardens to shame. Swaths of sheer material draped down from the ceilings, peppered with twinkling lights. Cloth-covered chairs with big bows that even Martha Stewart would envy. K.'s dream was coming true....and so was my nightmare. I felt like a conspicuous black ink stain in this sea of frothy, princess pink and white. Though dressed and coiffed appropriately, I nevertheless might as well have been Goth Girl/Death Rocker Barbie, inadvertently stumbling into Skipper's Cheerleading world of AWESOMENESS!

How many glasses of wine could I secretly chug before my father started giving me the evil eye or I slurred my way through the toast? I decided wisely to pace myself...it would be a long night. It had been a long year and soon...K. would be off on her honeymoon and I could safely and creatively implement one of the many imagined escape routes from this miserable life that I'd kept on reserve in the back of my rotting brain to end the daily pain I was in...preferably without leaving room for the inevitable postmortem gossip sessions I had now narrowly avoided...

"...and that's how her selfish, suicidal sister ruined K.'s most important and special day...can you believe it? Like she couldn't just wait a few days/weeks/months more to off herself in the garage? What a total BITCH!"

I wanted to wait until she was safely on a plane headed back home from somewhere tropical so I didn't ruin either the wedding or the subsequent honeymoon. Very thoughtful of me I figured. Basic courtesy, really. I hoped I'd be able to wait.... it would all depend on the next few weeks and how much post-wedding fallout I could stand before exiting stage left.

"Hey maid of honor...you look great...how are you doing?" my lifelong friend Amy, eight and three quarters' months pregnant and about to pop, waddled over to give me a hug.

"Hangin' in there...how are YOU doing?" I looked at her watermelon midsection and thought her a hero to come out on such a stormy night when tens of others had bailed using the foul weather as their excuse.

"Peter and I wouldn't miss it...you and K. are like sisters to me, you know that..." she said...Looking at her ripe belly and at my sister in her gown I knew that these were things I'd never experience...a day of love declarations, a life beating inside me. A lump the size of Donald Trump's ego, and tickling like it had his combover, too, popped up in my throat...

"Can I get you a ginger ale or something?" I asked her...not wanting to finish the last conversation we'd ever have even though the photographer was waving me over impatiently.

"No—I'm fine...you better go do your thing." She nodded in the general direction of the head table...or as I like to refer to it...nightmare spot where 200 people can watch you eat onstage for entertainment. I took my Trump lump and lurched over to the sadist with a camera who would capture my spare tire and ridiculous Shirley Temple ringlets and immortalize them forever on film.

I did my thing. I trudged over and took pictures dutifully. I gave my toast dutifully. I held up my sister's train dutifully. I stayed mostly sober dutifully. I danced dutifully. I avoided running screaming and sobbing to the ladies' room during the bouquet toss dutifully. I spoke to relatives dutifully. Autopilot engaged....keep on moving...just like a shark...if you stop, you're dead. You're dead anyway, but let's let the nice people eat their wedding cake first before we make funeral arrangements...mmmm'k? This was the last day on the job. Might as well go through the motions of returning phone calls and taking down pictures and putting plants in a box before you head out the door, go home and consume massive amounts of pills washed down with massive amounts of booze. I didn't know how I'd gotten here. I only knew I wanted to go home. And home...was not my parents' house. Home was somewhere else entirely...Little did I know that I'd end up in A HOME....As in a home for crazies.

It pays to be specific. God, clearly a former cheerleader herself, has a very mean sense of humor sometimes and that old 'be careful what you wish for' thing is more true than not. Just when you think you are balancing daintily on the top of the pyramid...someone will come along, look up your skirt, point, laugh and then push you off cackling as you tumble to the ground, skirt up around your ears and a breeze cooling off your nether regions. Exposed for all the world to see. And photograph.

Welcome to the Pines Pavilion...will you be staying long?

You can get there from here

My friend L. came to visit me about the third week of my 6-month stay at a hospital and treatment facility known for its beautiful grounds and former celebrity clientele. I'd been told that it wasn't uncommon for it to take 6 months or longer to get properly diagnosed and find the right medication combo. By the time L. showed up, I was about fed up with the ECT, looked and felt the worst I had in my life and was alternately comforted and ashamed to have a visitor, even one I'd known since I was 13 years old. L. was and is a compassionate and empathetic soul who had seen me through my college senior slump, countless breakups, unrequited crushes, job losses and numerous mini-breakdowns along the way. To be fair—I'd been there for her during many three-Kleenex, two ice-cream pint crises, too. We were closer than sisters but when she saw me with stringy, unwashed hair, dark circles under my eyes sporting the blue and white hospital bracelet—(it wasn't exactly Tiffany's) I could tell she saw only the stranger who had replaced her vibrant friend and partner in crime. The saddest part of this time for me was not really being able to recall who came and went—the steady stream of friends bringing flowers, cards, little gift baskets. The ECT gave me an amnesia that was completely random and embarrassing. I'd read over the cards and have no recollection of when I'd seen this friend or that and what our visit had been like. Having always had a sort of savant talent for remembering friends' numbers, addresses, birthdays and telling details, I suddenly forgot even their last names or how we'd originally met. And I'm talking lifelong friends in some cases. It was distressing and difficult to disguise. I must've seemed like the stereotypical drooling mental patient who was so overmedicated that she didn't even remember her own name let alone what day/year it was or who the President was—common questions asked by the nursing staff to check our lucidity levels. I'd often feign that I didn't know who the President was and then grudgingly admit that I preferred to block that little tidbit of information out, thanks very much.

One thing I can say with conviction is that the other 'clients' had a dark sense of humor that was like a salve to the jagged soul. 'Patients' was suddenly an outdated term leaving me to wonder if we were 'clients' what exactly were we consumers of? Mental health I suppose and a boatload of pharmaceuticals…I took up smoking for the camaraderie of the smoke breaks and figured if I couldn't kill myself quickly—slowly would be acceptable until other options opened up. My fellow immature inmates and I relished the invisible 'us' vs. them' battle between the key holders and the pill poppers. We were society's rebels and misfits while they were the put-upon, martyred burnouts with all of the power (mainly the keys to freedom) it seemed. Smoke breaks were daily opportunities to pick apart their flaws since we felt sick of them picking apart ours. It was like a water cooler where the officemates diss upper management and gossip about them was a bonding technique that we'd perfected. Our misdirected anger kept our pride intact and preserved what tiny remnants of pitiful dignity we could cling to in a place that proved that 'hell' was in fact not an abstract term. But—hell had a TV and lots and lots of cookies. With an eye towards nutrition, some of the eating disorder girls avoided the kitchen like the plague while those on certain antidepressants gravitated towards sugar like crack-addicted prostitutes looking for their next fix/trick.

I'd never been one of those lucky people who lost their appetite while depressed, however—even with a deep and abiding love of food I was not one to eat like it was my job either. I am not a petite girl. Wearing a size 12/14 at 5'9", weight had always been an issue for me. It had never gone to either extreme of starvation or bulimia like it did for my sister and lots of female friends over the years. While I'd tried every diet on the planet since the age of 12, I just couldn't stand the sensations of gagging or gnawing hunger so it seemed I was doomed to be 'chubby, zaftig, voluptuous or heavy'...while friends claimed that my height disguised many sins I have seen the pictures and do actually own a mirror or two. But seeing these skin and bones skeletal girls who would alternate between cutting an apple into a thousand tiny pieces one day and eating tons of junk food and soda the next, I actually felt grateful for my curves. Sure my belly was soft and I'd always been and always would be calorie-conscious—but fat was not the main source of my misery. No woman on this planet in this century can escape body image issues. It's all been said and all of the arguments have been made so I won't even go into this issue further except to say that when they do finally wise up and invent fat-blasting chocolate chip cookies and chub melting ice cream—I will be the first to buy stock.

But no matter what issues someone might have—be it schizophrenics talking to their imaginary friends, (auditory hallucinations) bipolars who could laugh one moment and be crying the next due to rapid cycling (mood swings), or depressives languishing in the sorrow of a world where life had lost its flavor (dysthymia)—we were all united against 'the man'. Intellectually, many of us knew on some level that most of our caregivers were dedicated, gentle-spirited professionals who must have good hearts to be working with such a broad range of neuroses, psychoses and other 'oses'. But that didn't help when we felt like trapped animals at the mercy of perceived enemies whose sole job it was to medicate us and get us to behave 'appropriately'. Most of us were there in the first place due to a life of being forced to behave appropriately and this was our only time to let loose from those constraints of trying to be normal and mainstream when inside we were anything but. Or at least that's what we secretly believed about ourselves whether it was true or not. Many of us, despite what people might think, had come from so-called 'normal' backgrounds while many more had come from hell only to return home again. It seemed you could get 'here' from 'there'. 'Here' being a place where time disappears, thoughts advance and retreat simultaneously and memories blur at the speed of light. Days blend together with only meals and pills and people to mark the hours. 'There' being a world just beyond reach where hope lives contentedly and keeps the carrot ever dangling. Where routine is sanity instead of insanity and where words like 'sanity' and 'insanity' are clearly defined. I just don't remember exactly when I had crossed the line between *here* and *there* except that I know my little sister's wedding had definitely been a landmark along the way.

The diagnosis that was finally settled upon was too clichéd and irritating for me to accept at first. Bipolar Disorder, formerly known as Manic Depressive Syndrome. Like Prince it had changed its name, apparently. Pretty soon there would just be some sort of symbol to represent it…maybe like a seesaw or something equally cheesy. I had a difficult time even saying the words without rolling my eyes. I argued that the nature of a human being is inherently bipolar—didn't we all have light and dark, good and bad, misery and joy in us? My astute psychologist noted: "Yes—but not everyone experiences them all so violently or to such extremes within the course of a day or a week". This was the same doctor who came to visit me in the hospital the week after my attempt, looking exhausted himself, who said that he would continue to treat me but that he couldn't treat me if I was dead. The man had some good points.

So I tried to listen—but still I argued and made my case that I thought this was a trendy diagnosis du jour and railed at how I was utterly horrified by the fact that kids—even toddlers were being slapped with this label and medicated. Popping pills before you can even read seems like a sanctioned form of child abuse. I believed it to be (and still do) fundamentally wrong and disturbing on so many levels. I was self-righteous and enraged. I was just a few indignant, obnoxious statements short of Tom Cruise. I loftily discussed my distaste for the term 'illness' and wanted to substitute 'wellness'—as in: *"My wellness level is not where I'd like it to be yet—but I'm working on increasing it"*. But I was still miserable. Then he made the very simple point (quoting Oliver Sachs) that I'll carry with me always:

"It's not the illness a person has that matters, it's the person the illness has that does." I could understand now—at least to some degree. He also talked about any illness being on a continuum and that everyone's symptoms were different. These seemed like obvious truths especially on a locked ward where I saw the parade of pain and of all its different masks. In a brief previous hospitalization about four years earlier I recalled that one patient had gotten some baby powder and made a paste of it smearing it all over his face and in his hair, wore a white hospital sheet (and nothing else) and waltzed around calling himself Moses asking us to 'let my people go' until he was ushered gently but firmly to that facility's version of the Quiet Room. Like a time-out for the naughty mentally ill people. Folks for whom no amount of happy vitamins would help.

Another crusade I took on in groups—discussing the nine million terms for people who were sick on a mental level rather than a physical one. We were categorized by the following words and phrases just to name a few: 'ape, barmy, batty, berserk, cracked, crazed, cuckoo, daft, delirious, demented, deranged, flaky, flipped, flipped out, freaked out, fruity, haywire, insane, kooky, lunatic, mad, maniacal, moonstruck, nuts, nutty, potty, psycho, screw loose, screwy, silly, touched, unbalanced, unglued, unhinged, unwell, wacky and my personal favorite—wacko. The list goes on...I was so angry at being marginalized. Language can be so limiting and cannot even begin to capture the flight of the soul and how some people can veer off the path sometimes. It was like an extra special combination of victimhood and underdog syndrome. So we used dark humor to disguise our underbubbling fear and anger. During my brief but memorable tenure on the locked ward, which ultimately totaled a month-long visit, there would be occasional reprieves and then a longer stay in a follow-up program—but a week here and there back on the ward added to about 35 days or so—who's counting? I was—you can be sure of that. I'd return—like many of the others on the infinity loop between the discharge transitional program to lockup when a medication had failed or during the early days of recovery when crisis seemed to lurk around every corner. Throughout these fragmented times, I'd sometimes see some young women sitting by the nurses station holding a frozen orange to 'get grounded' so they wouldn't cut themselves or purposely throw up. At those moments I would despair, thinking that maybe society was right...we couldn't function on the outside world it seemed let alone in the 'safe' hospital environment. We all, for our different reasons, wanted to fly away, leaving our bodies and our lives behind. Surely there were a few who fought to recover some will to survive, to continue, to slay their mental dragons and quiet their emotional demons.

I was scared enough to try and be in the survivor category most of the time. I was loved enough to find the tiniest slivers of hope in the oddest corners. But what of the burn victim who had red slits for eyes and seared, scarred flesh from the top of her wispy balding head to the soles of her flaking feet? I was humbled by and full of compassion for her and wondered why, if she could try and live why couldn't I? But it wouldn't last, couldn't last. I was no Christopher Reeve it seemed. Friends visited always seeming nervous and twitchy and very downhearted to see me 'in a place like this'. They swore they'd 'had no idea' that I was struggling so much and for so long. After awhile, faces blended together and I found that my role became to reassure them. That it would be ok, I'd be ok...and things would get better. And those times I couldn't keep it up I wept for hours or days until my tears dried up and I was exhausted and emotionally spent. Growing up, people often called me 'too sensitive' or sometimes 'a crybaby' accusing me of 'pulling crocodile tears'. I could no more easily stifle those tears than I could transform into an actual crocodile. I was not born an actress, I was made one when it became abundantly clear early on that difficult feelings were not tolerable. Sadness or anger or anything perceived as 'self-pity' or 'pouting' had a very short half-life in our family until these emotions were pushed underground before they even had a chance to breathe or be identified as such. I suspect we were not alone in this—it was the 'legacy' (to coin my sister's term) of the middle-class, of stoic New Englanders, of Irish Catholic Americans a generation removed. Unlike in the old country with Keats and Joyce, here in the good ol' U.S. of A, melancholy was a luxury we could not afford—false cheer was much more preferable to authentic sorrow. The irony being that the falsity ultimately took more energy and did more long-term damage than did a good, healthy keening session.

I quickly learned that heritage had nothing to do with it, really, though. It cut across regional, gender, cultural, race and age lines with a ruthless abandon. In group therapy I heard unimaginable horror stories of negligence, abuse, molestation and other atrocities that I couldn't wrap my brain or stomach around. Pain has no color, taste, ruler to measure by or words enough to capture its ability to steal spirit and wear one down to a soul nub. I was blessed in comparison to many of the people who had survived things far worse than I had. I should've felt grateful. So why did I envy terminally ill people their will to fight for survival while I could barely summon the energy to get out of bed for weeks and months at a time? I had my physical health—but my emotions and thoughts were enemies of my mind and their weapons were shadowy doubts echoing loudly and incessantly at 3am. I know family members and friends sometimes grew impatient with me as they feared I might never get well or snap out of my 'wallowing' and I grew even more impatient with myself.

Over time and with the tenacity of a loving support network who simply would not give up no matter how much I begged them to let me go—I found my feet stepping tentatively at first and then with gaining strength on the path to healing. It took intensive therapy; cocktails of drugs tried and rejected; a shock and awe attack on my central nervous system and hearing the stories of the fellow broken people to slowly renew my hope. Because in the end I realized that we weren't broken—just badly bruised. I met some of the most courageous, kind, creative, generous of heart, brilliant, wacky, funny, tragic and annoying people I have ever encountered during my time in the 'bin'...We called it the bin because it empowered us to destigmatize the word. To make light of our darkness. In England—a 'bin' is the trash—and in lots of ways were were throwaways, considered weak, leeches of society, losers and rejects who couldn't hold down a job or get our act together, quitters who ran out on relationships and responsibilities. When I think of the harsh way the world judges someone who has crossed the line of eccentricity just a bit too far and has embodied all of their greatest fears...it makes me want to weep all over again. For the sheer lack of understanding, education, and ignorance that allows Prozac jokes to still continue...Newsflash: If you aren't on Prozac or some form of psychiatric med—you can be assured that someone in your family or inner circle is... It might be perceived as terribly strong to go through life without the 'crutch' of medicine or talk therapy. I know strength. Strength is different for everyone. Pride is not strength. Ignorance is the true weakness. Getting help is strong. Needing help is not weak. Needing help and not getting it? Now that's just plain crazy.

Last One on the Ark is a Rotten Egg!

Ugh--the horrors and terrors of the modern dating scene! From Holly Go-Lightly and Helen Gurley Brown to Bridget Jones, society is relentlessly fascinated by the phenomenon that is the single, never-married woman. Images range from free-spirited independence and perpetual party girl to that cardigan-sporting, eccentric old spinster woman on the hill surrounded by a circus of cats. There really isn't much of a male equivalent apart from the aging bachelor who eats TV dinners and never has clean, or for that matter, matching socks. In the Noah's Ark scenario, there are lots of leftovers who've never chosen the two-by-two path—loneliness doesn't discriminate by gender. However, being a single never-married woman, I can only speak to what I know. And what I know is that being single can be the suckiest, most depression-inducing thing or it can sometimes be sort of ok. But for me, it was a large contributing factor to the overwhelming loneliness that drove me closer and closer to the edge. As my baby sister's wedding went from her early childhood fantasy playacting with Barbie and Ken to a grown-up version reality, I reviewed the other weddings I'd attended and realized that this was starting to take its toll on me more than I could've ever imagined.

All of my female friends but one or two holdouts are, or have been married. Countless times, I've attended nuptials ranging in style and budgetary limits. While one wedding boasted the swan ice sculpture and night reception at the Aquarium overlooking the starlit bay, another took place in an old barn, which still had the scent of hay in the air. Perhaps the least formal was a summer BBQ wedding where both Bride and Groom wore shorts and sandals. My favorite image from that particular occasion was the very large and very contented woman toking on a cigar, cooling her feet in a baby pool. I've welled up as friends joined their lives to soul mates in some lucky cases and to those who would be cellmates in the prison of an unhappy union.

There certainly are advantages and disadvantages to both the single and attached lifestyles. Case in point, the attached woman with PMS has someone to beat up on whereas the single woman has only herself and her funhouse distorted reflection in an evil mirror. And all mirrors are evil at that particular time of the moon's cycle. Single and attached women everywhere will lament about the 50 extra mystery pounds that appeared virtually overnight, crave exotic concoctions like movie popcorn with peanut M&Ms, and cry at car commercials. The difference of course being that the attached woman has a convenient target to aim her righteous feminine anger towards. The obvious candidate is the poor schlub who fell in love with Ms. Jekyll (the lovely MD) never dreaming that Mrs. Hyde (the scary psychopath) is lurking in the shadows ready to pounce. But by this point he's hooked, doomed and if he's smart he will have an arsenal of Ben and Jerry's stashed at the ready for just such an occasion.

Single women, on the other hand, are in effect, "shooting blanks" on a monthly basis. A rather crude way of saying that to add insult to injury, some of us know that every Tampax leads us closer into the dreaded arms of the infertility monster who stands at the end of a long, lonely road, brandishing the biological ticker in one grotesque claw and a picture of your mother's bereft and baffled *"Where are my grandchildren?"* face in the other.

Which reminds me of the old joke,

> **Q.** *"Why do single heterosexual women and gay men get along so well?"*
>
> **A.** *"They are both used to being a disappointment to their parents."*

By no means considered un-cute (as we've established), I have had a many a beau in my day. My insecurities forced me to write that last sentence lest my dear reader be musing that I am merely one more neurotic, dateless and desperate freak seeking sympathy. That's society's undertone of pitying embarrassment for and ultimate nagging fear of the enigma that is the unattached woman talking, folks. As I've observed pals getting on the marriage merry-go-round and joining the baby parade (to say nothing of the homeowner hullabaloo) I still rank among those who rent. Renting is a bit like dating in that both are an investment of sorts and a risk, too. Both activities can pay off in different ways. You get the joys of companionship and shelter without the headaches of shackles or mortgages. Perfect for the commitment-wary. You get to try on the energies of people and places and hope for a match without putting your heart or pocketbook into too much trouble.

Is it better to have loved and lost or to stay in and order a pizza? People are always saying that love is a game and there are rules of attraction. I am not nor have I ever been a player when it comes to matters of the heart. As far as I can tell, the golden rule is the only worthwhile one anyway and all the rest is so much smoke and mirrors. I've always maintained jokingly of course, but half seriously.... I will be the old lady surrounded by cats when my demise comes knocking its grisly finger upon time's door. But I hope in my inner heart that this is just self-deprecation at its finest and not a self-fulfilling prophecy.

I've been in the gut wrenching, soul twisting kind of love and I've been in the fondness/affection/sweetness kind of love, too. I've even had the kind of love where the two of you are as thick as thieves and as innocent as toddlers giggling on joy juice until dawn. Then in between these loves I have rested, licked my wounds and readied myself for the back-on-the-horse times when love rallies and surprises you just when you had been eyeing those cat condos lustily.

One thing I have learned over time is that love cannot and should not be forced. If two people are moving in entirely different directions and begin speaking in tongues to try and save a drowning rat love it is a sad and lonely thing to behold. Because love should enhance your freedom to be yourself, your best, worst and in-between self. What qualifies me as the love guru all of a sudden? I have never even had a relationship that lasted beyond 2 years and I am preaching to the masses? I've got eyes don't I? I can see love wither and die and miraculously be reborn out of ashes that smolder between two passionate people. I know it's not the same as being in it. That's why I have kitty plan B since I am clearly not an aficionado at this whole love shebang dealio.

But I still have hope, some of which was rekindled by seeing the spouses and significant others of the other hospital residents. They didn't care what pills their sweethearts had to take to feel better—they just loved them and wanted them to be around for a very long time. I saw such supportive people and it made me realize that what I would bring to a future relationship was more than the 'baggage' I feared. I was and am a multidimensional person with lots to offer and oh yeah—my brain juice is kinda fucked up but I'm managing that just like a diabetic manages their insulin levels. In fact—I am the one who's foolishly picky so if I meet a guy I think won't be accepting of my situation it's sayonara and don't let your ass touch my door on the way out—my door's too good for you. But you've gotta give people a chance sometimes, right? I have a friend who has a One-Date theory. It goes something like this: no matter how bright, dull, tall, short, bald, fat, skinny, bulging-eyed, knock-kneed or pigeon-toed a guy is—she will grant him one date. I commend her for her saint-like quality—I am a tad more selective when it comes to choosing who I will choose to spend an hour in a coffee shop with or over a meal discussing my last four relationships or why I decided to major in Spanish and then never use it again after college. That always stumps people into utter baffled and bewildered silence. Anyway—things that might normally be dealbreakers for some of us, she will overlook and date just for the fun and socialization and the 'what if he could be, might be, may be my lobster' factor? She has a lot of good stories from these dates. But not one 'real' romance has bloomed from any of them. Or at least not one that counted or mattered to her in any lasting, memorable way. Yes—I know—it's good experience, good practice, etc. Steaming pepperoni baby...!

I have set the bar impossibly high due to having grown up with parents who have loved each other essentially since they were born (junior high, high, school era) and are still together, remain each other's best friends and are very much in love to this day after knowing each other's every quirk, facial tic and speech pattern. That, my friends, is a hard legacy to top. Hence the seemingly unreachable standards I have for Mr. X. And I know my parents struggled to keep their love alive. They worked hard at it and never gave up on each other or the relationship. At times, I thought this was stupid and codependent and I would roll my eyes at their naivete about the social constraints of marriage and how unnatural it is for humans to pair off for 50+ years and never veer off course. I'm sure they veered and refocused and kept that pattern going out of habit or fear or what was that thing again? Oh yeah—everlasting love. That doesn't just happen in fairy tales—I know this from 30+ years of knowing them. Perhaps I was the naive one and still am. But I am still finding my way in this love game even as the rules change every day. And I respect my friend's advice but I know that in choosing a mate to spend 50+ years with there has to be a mutual attraction, intellectual stimulation, sense of humor and the capacity for arguing in a constructive way. And the other ingredient that my parents both agree on wholeheartedly after 40 years together—chemistry. Without that any relationship is doomed.

You can't build chemistry--it's there or it isn't. I am realizing that open-heartedness and open-mindedness are the most desirable qualities I can cultivate in myself while I dabble in the One-Date theory, all the while reserving the chance to die surrounded by grandchildren who love me instead of the imagined and dreaded multiple feline critters who crawl nonchalantly over my corpse to get to the kitty litter. I am sure there is some scenario in between and hopefully that day is a long way off and I will be lucky enough to have some fun on the way. In the meantime—I may just be ok by myself with a good book, a phone call from a friend and getting out in the world every now and then to mingle and try again. And I suppose it's lucky for me that I'm not overly fond of cats after all...

When I turned 30, I succumbed briefly to panic. Part of me lectured sternly. *"OK, time to grow up now."* And then off to the nearest tattoo parlor I headed to do something totally out of character and allow a stranger to stick needles with ink in my lower back to create a beautiful image of a multicolored butterfly. Who says I can't commit? That sucker is going to the grave with me, thanks very much. For me, the butterfly symbolized the struggle to come out of a cocoon and fly. Unfortunately, long after the ink dried and the snide comment from my lovely smartass dad who wisecracked, *"When does it wash off?"*; it seems a few years later my wings are still wet and clearly I have one or two remaining web-bish strands to break through. I've met other people in my age group and beyond who are all in their varying stages of transition and transformation (and not all during my 'retreat' either). I must admit--this comforts me in some strange way. We misfits have a way of finding each other through the mist. We are life's round pegs who don't all fit into square lives or cubicles. I'm not criticizing those who prefer walls and corners to define their boundaries. After all, it could be said of the circle that it's simply the shape of one creature—whether canine or human—endlessly chasing its own tail.

My path has definitely had its derailing detours, (understatement) but I've also known moments of pure bliss, shed both tears of joy and sorrow, gotten to know myself better, shared my bed and my heart but lately I've slept alone and been ok with it. It's alright, really. No need to wrinkle your brow in sympathy or rack your brain for eligible bachelors to set me up with...I'll confess that sometimes it totally sucks, but mostly it's fine. Yes, I do want to share my life and grow old with someone special. Yes, I too, want the white wedding and maybe even the white fence someday. But for now, I wear black, not because I'm in mourning, but because it's chic *and* slimming.

Shut Your Smart Mouth

In our house my mother, was generally the disciplinarian and groundings were her specialty. She claims I have a selective memory but my childhood friends back me up on this point. I missed several birthday parties and after school trips to the mall as well as a concert or two due to my 'fresh mouth'. This talent for back-talking is one that only a teenager can hone over years of prepubescent building resentment. Once the hormones hit, every single sarcastic comment in every single strand of DNA worms its way up into the esophagus and into the mouth, releases and hits the air, oftentimes before the recipient (usually the parents of said teenager) or even the teenager herself know what is happening. Inevitably these smartass remarks are followed by the knee-jerk parental response to *"Go to your room"*. Which is usually code for: *"Get out of my sight before I am forced to kill you right here, right now, as we both know that I am capable of--so it would be quite smart for you to take your smart mouth out of slapping range because I feel my arm wanting to go there as though pulled by some magnetic force."*

It's an age-old dance done for centuries, really. Luckily, I was born after the Salem witch trials and public canings because there is no doubt in my mind that my 'smart mouth' would've caused me no end of grief then, too. As it was, in suburbia, in the seventies one got the occasional spanking (as a toddler), slapped (as a preteen) and in a few cases, in my house there was a sort of upping the ante in the teen years. I can remember one major incident when I was about 14 or so. A friend had let me borrow her bike to ride it home and when I got there the tension in the house clearly hung in the air. That 'post-fight' tension that I was almost used to where your stomach locked and breath stopped the minute you walked in the door, your body knowing what has transpired before your brain can register it. Since about age 12, my parents' marriage had been in a 'rough patch' as they called it, complete with closed-door whisper fights that often escalated into louder, scarier episodes. I was not in the mood for their bullshit. I was almost fourteen and sick of them fighting all the time and saying the most horrible things to each other.

So when my mother, scheming up some reason to leave the house no doubt, told me we were going shopping for winter boots and to 'get in the car', I flatly refused. This, needless to say, did not go over well since my father had just told me to return my friend's bike and I had also flatly refused him saying that I would do it later. I didn't want to be in the middle of their tug of war and was tired of feeling like they were the teenagers and so I stood my ground. Defiance is the sword and shield of the hormonally challenged teen and I was exercising my battle cry.

My father is one of those slow-to-burn and then explode types. His temper is typically Irish American (with decades of tempers preceding it) and frightening and you do not want to be in its path. There were not many violent outbursts, perhaps a half dozen or so that I remember, throughout my childhood and adolescence, like the one that ensued but when they did happen they were both baffling and terrifying...mostly to him, I think. He flew into a rage the likes of which I'd only seen on the nature channel when a predator pounced on its prey.

When in the grip of these mini-hurricanes, his face looked like it might literally leave his head and start shooting out in all directions....an eyeball here, teeth there. He dragged me to the door by my shirt collar kicking and screaming...he kicking, me screaming, all the while swearing at me and telling me that I would listen godammit and that he was sick of my know-it-all attitude. I was to return the bike and then go to the mall for the boots and that was the end of it.

I sobbingly returned the bike propping it on its kickstand by my friend's fence, too embarrassed to knock and tell them I was bringing it back and I walked home wondering what awaited me there. I remember feeling that death wish numbness for the first time. The same numbness that I'd feel 20 years later sitting in the car in the garage. I desperately wanted to die. And not in the '*I'm almost fourteen and I hate my parents and everything sucks so they'll come to my funeral and be sorry then*' kind of wanting to die. It was simply an overwhelming curiosity about what death held and a fear that maybe it was better for all of us if I were to just not exist. I think everyone's felt this way at low points in their lives but I didn't know that then. When I finally admitted defeat and went to the mall with my mother I just remember melodramatically saying to her in the car, "*I hope you're happy now that your husband just beat the shit out of me*". The fact was there wasn't a bruise or scratch on me and it was mostly my psyche that had absorbed the impact of the blows. Somehow in all of my youthful wisdom I was convinced it was *her* fault, she was the one he was really angry with so I declaimed him as my father and he became a stranger who was just married to my mother because surely nobody who shared my blood could've been so cruel and violent. I made it clear that I was not going to shop for boots or anything else and stayed in the car for almost two hours while she went in and pretended to kill time. The entire two hours was filled with funeral fantasies and images of me opening the car door and walking out into the nearby traffic in front of a Mack truck. I imagined the old cartoon images of someone being flattened by a steamroller. Like rolling out pie dough...with a shoe flying in the air for dramatic effect.

Cartoons aside, I knew didn't want to be part of this family anymore, or part of this life. I wanted to be in a family where everyone didn't know the charming public persona father version of Dr. Jekyll and tell you how wonderful he was all the time, this same man who behind closed doors could be the ticking time bomb 'Mr. Hyde' who punched and kicked and spit like a cornered animal and then seemed to conveniently block it out afterwards like the whole thing had been completely normal and you were the one who was overreacting. I think that was the most damaging part of these rare but extreme incidents. Not their frequency, intensity or aftermath--no visible cuts or bruises ever appeared...it was the denial that surrounded them. He tried so hard to make up for it, to be a good father, to be present when he could in his own way. But never acknowledging these episodes of rage and pain was more scarring than 1st degree burns to the soul. It was only years later as an adult that I could tell him that as a 6'4" 225-lb. man his mere physical presence was scary and that I had felt afraid of him and that my stomach went into knots whenever I'd see him getting angry. I think the shame he feels and felt over this was equal to my shame at having tried to commit suicide. The difference is I don't want to pretend it never happened because then I'm afraid it might happen again. Not that the hitting or verbal abuse would happen in reality, but that I'll keep replaying it over and over in my head until I allow myself to believe it was true and not a figment. Not just some invisible storm that ravaged us all but left no visible mark. So I'm opening my smart mouth. Because I never want to be in a car in a garage waiting for death to steal me away again.

Have I forgiven my father for his early rages? Well, I can say this. I am trying my best to do so and I'm almost all the way there. I know he got help for his anger issues and I know he had a high-pressure career and a tumultuous relationship with my mother at times. In a forty-year marriage those 'rough patches' are to be expected. And I'm not a teenager anymore, not living under his roof or his rules. We are different creatures he and I, but the same in many ways. It is a complicated love, twisted up with fear and shame and adoration and disappointment. And I do honor and respect him for what he's been able to achieve and accomplish in his life and I do know that he would give his life for his family. But I'm tired of protecting him and tired of feeling like I'm 'crazy' and that these things never happened or were some exaggerated creation of my overactive imagination. They did. It was traumatic for all involved. We all survived and became stronger and yes, even 'smarter' because of it. And wisdom or healing that is so hard won is the only kind worth having in the end. But when it hurts so much that you can't feel the hurt anymore and the forgiveness comes and goes with the memories, then you have to speak up and be open about the fact that yes, every family has problems, and no, it may not be the kind or fair thing to 'air your dirty laundry' but it is the truth. And everybody will have their version of it and that's as it should be. I can only tell my version as I mentioned before. He has his version. I can never really know his way of seeing it since even after years of family therapy he skirts the issue and can't seem to go there in any deep or meaningful way. In his eyes the past is the past and it's over. There's no point in rehashing or reliving it over in this way. Speaking it aloud (or in this case writing it for all and sundry to read) is breaking the cardinal rule of family silence and breaching a sacred trust—the ultimate disloyalties. He's entitled to that point of view. I happen to disagree. And now, the progress we've made is that disagreement does not have to end in tears or disaster. For that I am truly grateful and my heart and my smart mouth agree for once.

Drinking Bleach is No 'Solution'

Aside from this lengthy hospital stay and my occasional teen angst episodes, I'd been strongly suicidal once in my late twenties about five years previous to the infamous garage incident. At that time, I'd also had horrible ongoing bouts with depression and insomnia but was more open about my suicidal ideations since it was the first time I'd ever experienced such total soul darkness and it scared the shit out of me. I told my parents and friends I was really struggling. They were sufficiently terrified when they asked how seriously I felt about killing myself and I told them that I'd gotten inches/minutes away from drinking a Clorox cocktail—was that serious enough for them? They convinced me to speak to a psychiatrist and her immediate suggestion was a brief hospitalization on a psych ward of a well-renowned medical hospital until the urgency of the crisis passed and a longer term care plan could be put into action. Since this particular hospital had a very good reputation I reluctantly agreed and packed an overnight bag figuring a few days' rest might be in order after all. When your laundry detergent starts singing a seductive siren song you get sufficiently freaked out and willingly hand yourself over to more knowledgeable care. I essentially slept for five days straight, spoke to one or two shrinks and a social worker in all of that time and was discharged with two prescriptions—one for an anti-depressant and the other stipulation was that I see both a psychiatrist (monthly) and a talk therapist (weekly) for no less than a year. As it turned out, this hospital was great if you needed surgery or cancer treatment but not so much on the mental illness stuff. The psych ward was clearly an afterthought. Sandwiched discreetly between terminal and shorter stay patient floors, it was a no-man's land and the protocol seemed to be drugs, sleep and quiet. Supernatural silence. Only occasionally disturbed by one or two random shouting, argumentative patients (for here we were still definitely 'patients' and not yet 'clients') for whom the library/morgue-like atmosphere was more unsettling than peaceful.

I don't remember much from that hazy, overmedicated time except feeling somewhat ignored and pissed off when one of the nurses told me that I was easily overlooked because I was so 'high-functioning'. Well—excuse me for taking up your time. No—please—go attend to the woman who is shedding her clothes and coming down from some kind of acid trip while I rot politely here in a corner contemplating new and wonderful ways to die. Go right ahead—we'll catch up later—ta ta...Have fun wrestling and calming her down—I might just tie the sheets together and hang myself from the shower pipe while you're gone but I'll try and be quick about it and I won't leave too much mess to clean up I promise. Blood would be too gory and require mops and such, so we'll just stick to suffocation or something dignified. After all—that's how we 'high functioners' like to operate. It was the fucking story of my miserable life, I felt. High functioning, high expectations, overachiever tendencies and ridiculously high bars always set just out of reach until I finally got tired of jumping. And the only kind of jumping I wanted to do now was off a bridge. Unless you were a junkie or an alkie (all due respect to the addiction-afflicted but I was in emotional crisis and very, very depressed remember?) or homeless, or sporting bloody scars, scabbed burns or screaming at the top of your lungs that you don't like chocolate pudding and verbally assaulting staff members—you were invisible. At first I enjoyed being under the radar and I just observed. Then I started to resent being hospitalized to get help and constantly patiently waiting my turn but realizing with growing horror that it might never arrive. It wasn't as though you took a number like at a bakery or deli...this was not first come, first serve. This was squeaky wheel time and there just wasn't enough grease to go around apparently. Unless you wore your pain visibly or were very um...vocal...about it then it didn't exist. Speak no evil, feel no evil. So I wrapped myself in the quiet blanket of sedation and sleep. When I did actually get to speak to someone I didn't really know what to say..."*Hi, I'm really sad...*" seemed just slightly inadequate.

Upon discharge though, I did feel quite a bit better--at least I had caught up on some much needed rest. With an action plan and my marching orders, I felt just the tiniest bit more hopeful that when I had professionals to work with on a one-to-one basis I might actually make some reasonable progress towards something resembling mental health. Or at the very least, bleach would start to just seem like a stain remover again and not the key to the doorway into the everlasting abyss.

The intake process to become a mental patient (client, whatever) is more rigorous than getting into an Ivy League University. There are more forms to fill out than the Army, Navy and Air Force combined. I spoke to no fewer than 10 people in four hours—all of whom asked the same questions so that I started to feel like the stereotypical snitch talking to the cops (*'I've already told you people time and again the same things over and over...'*) and that they were all comparing notes somewhere trying to see if my story didn't match up somehow. The worst thing was a mere 19 hours earlier when I had been reading the bottle of bleach's ingredients, had I known what excruciating interrogations lay ahead I probably would've just chugged away happily. It was exhausting, humiliating and I started to feel like it was a government experiment to see how long it took to break a person's spirit or drive a borderline sane person over an irretrievable edge. I'm sure I made some off-the-cuff joke to that extent and now have 'paranoia' forever listed as one of my diagnoses. See? I'm even paranoid about being called paranoid by a para-professional. That was the other thing—most of the interviewers were younger than me. Yeah—that's reassuring. Hi—I'm 28, you're 25 what worldly wisdom about not offing myself can you offer?

Sometimes, during these never-ending intake interrogations, the inquisitioners would try to strike a chatty note. Under other circumstances I might appreciate their casual breeziness, but I was utterly exhausted—drained both mentally and emotionally not to mention physically since carbon monoxide gives a hell of a hangover...and all I wanted to do was sleep for about four hundred years--not chat about who my favorite musicians were. Finally, after speaking to my last and creepiest 'whitecoat' as we came to think of them, I was checked into Hotel California—such a lovely place. The last guy almost had me walking out the door because between each question he would stare off into space and there would be these long, uncomfortable silences while he apparently mentally journeyed to Mars as I recounted the story of my life for the ten thousandth time. But the icing on the fruitcake was when he asked if apart from this situation, would I generally consider myself to be a happy person? I had to physically restrain myself from pinching him to see if he was real or made of wax.

Wax Man passed me onto the nurses' station where I was issued a very scratchy bleach-smelling (ironically) set of towels, a plastic-wrapped toothbrush, a one-inch thick pillow and some blankets that were holier than St. Mary herself. I was led down the corridor to the room I'd be sharing with pentagram/Goth girl—who actually turned out to be very nice and fell into a 15-hour, mercifully dreamless sleep. Only to be awakened by the aforementioned human alarm clock with the annoying mantra of "*C'mon, c'mon people—get up—we don't have all day—it's time to get up now!*" But we **did** have all day. None of us had important meetings to attend or carpools to drive or lattes to stand in line for...we had all the time in the world it seemed. But meds—ah—yes—wake up to take a pill that will sedate you...that made perfect sense. It was all about structure and routine and the importance of adhering to a schedule. Ugh. Where's the joy in that? What happened to restoring one's health by the ocean or in the mountains? I must've read Heidi one too many times growing up. We did actually have meetings to attend—goals setting in the morning and recap at night with a few options in between. You could sleep or do Yoga, sleep or create something colorful and glittery in Art Therapy, sleep or discuss Relationship Roadblocks, sleep or read in a corner quietly or sleep, sleep and sleep some more. For the first few days after a newbie is admitted, it is understood that they will be sleeping more than participating in any activities. After months of insomnia—I suddenly slept like it was an Olympic sport. I did have a lot of nightmares. I was never really refreshed and I was always, always exhausted.

We all know the most often blurted and least appreciated foot-in-mouth comment... *"You look tired..."* Well—I got that from everyone—friends, family, nurses, doctors...you name it—they all said it. I did not need to hear it—the mirror told me volumes. I not only looked tired—I looked like a hag who had lived hard and who was past her prime. I barely recognized myself and I remember one day just sobbing at my own reflection wondering if I had succeeded in killing myself after all as this shell of my former self looked back at me. I was tested for anemia and showed a borderline case of it which could account for some of the paleness and lack of energy. Suddenly a multivitamin with iron popped up in my daily morning med cup and little by little I started to feel and look more human and less like a creature-double-feature attraction. I have no doubt that the smoking and lack of proper nutrition weren't exactly enhancing my appearance situation either. Clearly my health was still not at the top of my priority list. Having a priority list was not on my priority list. Getting through the day without screaming my head off in frustration at what my life had come to was an achievement. Getting through the day with some distractions and a few laughs in the blackness? —Priceless.

Such a lovely place, such a lovely face

People are always telling me their dramas, troubles, stories and complaints. I'm talking complete strangers. Recently, I was in a checkout line and the woman who was ringing me up started volunteering information about her facial rash and how she thought it was impetigo--a highly contagious form of the yuckies. And as she was bemoaning her plight I couldn't help but think to myself, *"Should she be handling money?"* and wondered how I would accept my change without actually touching her. Does crazy recognize crazy? Do our genes have energetic, magnet-like transmitters that activate to attract like to like when it comes to weirdness? I asked someone once after they had launched into a woeful diatribe after having only met me ten minutes earlier, if she was always this revealing with everyone? And she said no, not really, apparently I just had 'that kind of face'...what kind of face? Did I catch the yucky rash? Oh, no, wait—mixing my stories, sorry. When I asked her what she meant she clarified. *"You know...like you'd be a good listener, open, kind."* I also get asked for directions a lot which is a real joke since I can get lost at the drop of a hat—not that I'd ever find the dropped hat—I'd be too busy being lost.

Clearly I had to start practicing my Dirty Harry expression if I wanted to get a moment's peace. I wanted to somehow remove the "Please unload here..." neon sign that seemed to be flashing on my forehead and apparently had been there since birth. Whether you call it being compassionate, empathetic, a weirdo magnet or even worse, 'sucker'...it all amounts to the same end result—hours of your life lost to boring people with their boring stories. Lots of friends have told me over the years that I should become a therapist and start charging for my advice. My rationale has been why study to learn how to do something you don't really want to do even though you may be gifted/cursed with an innate ability or talent for it? And then there's the whole getting depressed by being around depressed people syndrome. This one fellow 'inmate' at the treatment program was a therapist who was so burned out on her patients' stories and pain and never-ending neediness that she had literally made herself sicker than some of her clientele. She shared with us that yes...being a therapist had its rewarding moments but most of the time it was truly unsung hero work and some days you just didn't have the strength to don the cape and save the day. And she was mourning the loss of a full-term miscarriage that had devastated her on such a core level that she feared she might never properly heal.

It's harder to heal when you know all the reasons why you 'should' go on...but you still simply just don't want to and you are secretly plotting how to dupe everyone into thinking that you're 'well' enough to be released on your own recognizance. Janet knew how to 'talk the talk' and was able to manipulate her way out and back home earlier than had been advised. Having been a therapist she knew exactly what to say and how to appear to the professionals so that they would see how much she was 'progressing'. Each day for a week, Janet would weep a little less and be more centered—exhibiting less staring off into space until she managed to work on her husband and social worker, wearing them down until they agreed to let her continue to recuperate at home. She was released and returned three days later wearing the same overalls she'd left in…seeming downcast and sheepish. She admitted that for three days she'd been in bed, spinning her wheels and thinking up ways to off herself. Who did she admit this to? Yup, you guessed it…little Miss Open-Faced me. It broke my heart wide open to see her come back feeling so defeated and ashamed, yet the relief was also palpable because though Janet wanted nothing more than to be reunited with her unborn child, she also knew that she couldn't leave her husband to manage the double grief that her suicide would inflict. She said she was having dinner one night and he smiled sweetly at her across the table and she burst into tears of shame and guilt at her own duplicity. Apparently he had that kind of face, too.

Whether this face of mine and all of its unconsciously welcoming gestures is a burden or a blessing, I'll never really know. It's the one I was born with and for the most part it has served me well. I'll never be good at poker. I have one of those faces that is so expressive that it's too hard to bluff worth a damn. Though I have always been pretty good at fooling friends and family that things are fine when they are not, the ones who truly know me will hear it in my voice or notice the slight trembling around my eyes or mouth that give me away when 'Fine' means anything but fine. I, too, can talk the talk and my words have often distracted people, or my laugh, or my ability to turn the conversation back to the other person and keep it there. Babies and kids seem to react well to me and smile easily or flirt openly. Recently in a restaurant at the table next to me, a five-year-old asked her mother for a 'piece of gum' after their meal…I turned around and made a disgusted face and said "*Pizza gum???—eww that's disgusting—I didn't see that on the menu…*" The five-year old cracked up…the mother looked at me like "*Thanks, now I'll never hear the end of that one…*" Each year I look at the mirror at the transformation that happens as I age a little bit here and there. Tiny crow's feet and smile lines are starting to show up and since I'm not a Botox girl I guess they are here to stay. When I'm 90 (God willing) and I look in the mirror and the woman looking back has creases and doughy hanging flappage…I'll know I have really lived—lived so much I've worn out the very skin that houses the spirit that animates the face that encourages strangers to share their woes and joys. For I do get both ends of the spectrum sometimes. And shades of grey in between, remember? And then I'll be playing checkers in a sunlit room with a pal across from me who is telling me how their bones ache and how the tapioca wasn't up to snuff today or how their daughter never visits them anymore. And I'll listen and nod and look into their eyes deeply, beyond the years seeing only the friend I've known forever who knows me, too. And I won't regret not perfecting my Dirty Harry. And I'll be grateful someday that I have that kind of face. The kind of face that puts people at ease. The kind of face that makes babies smile and giggle with unbridled joy. The kind of face that sometimes looks pretty ok even without makeup. I will be glad that I have heard all the stories and the complaints and the absurdities that make us all human. After all…we all have that kind of face, really. We just don't always know it.

Goodnight Irene

Since the bipolar apple doesn't fall from the cuckoo tree, it's safe to say that mine aren't the only chemistry-challenged brain cells in the genetic soup that preceded me. I have an aunt and a great aunt who were both diagnosed with this lovely affliction as well. My aunt is the one who told me about my great aunt Irene. Apparently she, too, was a writer—a poet whose nerves were easily frazzled and who sadly spent the last several years of her life institutionalized. So along with our penchant for suicidal ideations and Shakespeare, we'd all logged some recovery time at 'spa retreats' where various different approaches spanned the generations and due to the advances in psychiatric treatment, I seemed to win the medication lottery. Lucky, lucky me. I still felt that the ECT I'd undergone was a throwback to medieval times—no matter how much research they had to back it up or how humane it is now that the patient is anesthetized, or how many people it's claimed to help—I still think it's a horribly primitive procedure at the core. And to this day I still thank the universe that I don't have to take lithium (which seems to work wonders for my aunt where it only made me feel like a complete zombie). No doctor can tell you why it works—it is a salt and apparently the most tried and true mood stabilizer. But who knows what they did to treat manic depression—as it was called then 70 years ago? I shudder to think.

Irene has long been somewhat of a mystery figure to me and all I really know of her are the bits and pieces passed down to me by my aunt, which doesn't amount to much in the end. I have one of her rings—a Peridot (given to me by the same aunt—at the time I wondered if by accepting it I was joining some sort of secret crazy society complete with decoder ring). I became leery and resentful of this woman I'd never even met. It was as though I was carrying a curse or something. Yet I was also curious about her. What had pushed her over the edge finally? Was she really so badly off that she had to be locked up for half of her life? Did she have friends? Lovers? Was she just eccentric or truly ill? Does anyone really know the difference anyway? Eccentric is what they call you if you are not a danger to yourself or others I suppose. 'Unwell' is an entirely different category altogether. Mostly, my powerful overriding feeling whenever I thought of her was the deep, unabiding fear that I would become her. Just like the old joke that a woman always turns into her mother—I wondered how far back that personality seed could go and waited for it to sprout. It definitely sprouted that day in the garage and hopefully it has been re-rooted and planted in healthier soil. Or at least that's what my therapist tries to tell me anyway. And I also like to go with the 'watered down' theory...as in: I have a much weaker version of what she had (and far more advanced treatment options) and even slightly diluted from my aunt's symptom manifestation as well. Of course, intellectually I know it doesn't work that way...We are all individuals and our genetically disposed health problems show up in different ways over time. And a diagnosis is just a label for a certain set of behaviors, blah, blah, blah. Treatment plans evolve over time as the miracle of modern science continually surprises us in new and fascinating ways. (ok—yes—it's hard for me to say that sans sarcasm)...But let's face it—some things never do change and heredity truly is the X factor in every family.

I can no sooner blame Irene for her faulty brain than I can claim Flipper as a distant relative. Though, since dolphins are apparently far more evolved in their brain waves than we piddling humans are—I'll take Flipper any day. But the interesting thing about those so-called rotting branches of the family tree is that they may bend to the breaking point and leave scars behind but they certainly help us understand the shadow side of life. And another huge lesson they teach us is compassion. And let's not forget patience. So when some lizard part of my mind flips out in its relentless hamster wheel spin and I know that even my medicine or talk therapy or deep breathing exercises are not helping, I take out the Peridot ring and give it a good cleaning. It's a weird homage to be sure but it's a small act of recognition nonetheless. I remind myself that she spent all that time locked up so I wouldn't have to. Her sacrifice was to the future generations of people who would come after, born of fragile and delicate mental stock. She's a beacon of guilty shame, blight on that apple that fell from that tree. But really she was just a woman, a woman, like me—who had an affinity for words.

The phrase I kept hearing over and over at the hospital was 'high functioning'—the doctors and staff members were always telling me how high functioning I was—as though I was some sort of computer that had lots of extra programs and features. I have the sneaking suspicion that Irene was not high functioning. I'm not sure which happened first—whether she gave up on life or life gave up on her. This little chicken and egg dilemma is at the heart of my question mark about her fate and how she got (and stayed) there. Was there a turning point? A snap, crackle and pop that occurred sending her into a twisted version of Never Never Land--never to return again? Or was it a more gradual progression building slowly and inevitably to a sad crescendo of living out her pre-golden and beyond years in a mental health facility? We all expect to log some time in some sort of institution when the euphemism 'assisted independent living' no longer applies and 'high risk for hip fracture and/or pneumonia' is the real state of affairs. But to spend the better part of the prime of your life there... plucked out of the flow of everyday life marking time only by meals and pills? Seems like the worst kind of living nightmare. I barely made it through 6 months let alone decades!

So when I think of her it is with empathy and horror. I feel for her and wonder if she'd found a committed (pun intended) psychologist like I was lucky enough to find—would she have been able to mainstream slowly back into the land of the living? Granted when I first met my psychologist I was beyond redemption I think. I'd begun seeing him a few months before my attempt. At that point, I believe my fate was sealed and unless he had been a complete miracle worker equipped with magic beans, no amount of talk therapy would or could have gotten through the muddy haze of pain I wore like a mantle. A few days before the garage episode, he had sent me to another doctor for a battery of tests to see if I had some sort of adult learning disorder type of thingy that would be a partial explanation as to why I was having challenges in work situations. I thought it absurd since I was a quick learner and able to sum up interoffice dynamics and people within three hours of being at any new job. However—there were lots of jobs that either I couldn't or wouldn't stick to and since it looked as though there was some sort of underlying self-sabotage playing out in this recurring pattern, he seemed to think these tests would help us find my particular strengths and deficits. So maybe Irene had inkblots and Freud—but I had the freakin' psychological SATs.

I mistrusted the testing doctor on sight. He managed to portray complete arrogance and embodied an air about him that relayed that clearly he had better things to do than waste his time with little old me....

"*Have a seat...*" he waved me in never looking up from the folder he was studying...notes on a previous client? The one after me? Had my doctor given him my chart?

He was doing this as a favor to my psychologist who was his colleague so he projected a '*let's go ahead and get this over with already*' attitude from the start. Yeah, nice bedside manner, pal. He asked me questions and I halfheartedly answered since I was having a horrible day and was highly distracted.

There were even a few inkblots, too.

"*You guys really still use those huh?*" I asked nervously. He glared at me as if I had just taken a dump in his morning oatmeal.

It was an unnerving experience--especially because his demeanor proceeded to get more and more condescending as the clock ticked interminably slowly. I couldn't even phone a friend or ask the audience for help with my final answers...it was Dr. Dickface and me with his fancy degrees on the wall and an ego that could dwarf Everest making it look like a cute little anthill. The clock was ticking louder than my heartbeat—which was drumming in my ears....thump-thump ticktock thumpthump ticktock...I can easily say that it was one of the longest hours of my life. At one point he even had a slight sneer and furrowed brow and he looked well—for lack of a better word—evil. He had moved from aloof and distracted into a more engaged and sadistic state. One of the answers I gave (I was officially sweating by now) must have played into his trap—he just looked at me with utter disgust and contempt as though he had asked me what 2 plus 2 was and I had answered 5,10000,999,77734. No doubt it was one of those Train A and Train B things that always send me into a near panic attack.

If I'd had an ounce of backbone or self-caring or protective instinct of any sort left I would (should) have gotten up and walked out. But I proceeded to let this man 'shrink' me in more than one sense of the word. When I was reduced to a milkweed fluff about to blow away in the wind, the test mercifully finally ended. I felt humiliated, stupid, angry and hopeless.

Clearly I was just too dumb to live. I mean—I knew I was 'intelligent'—I'd always gotten good grades and the feedback from friends and former coworkers, teachers and bosses was that I was articulate, funny and bright. But knowing that did not help. Dr. Hitler had shredded me in one hour with his little stained cards and poker face. I didn't even have the energy to hate him. That came later.

Two days later I was in the car, in the garage, in my own very personal and awful ring of hell. I can't blame the Dumbass Dictator Doc. He was only a small piece of the last straw phase and his crappy stupid test and single raised, *"Have you always been slow?"* eyebrow was only a catalyst for a plan set in motion years before. But sometimes when I think of Irene—I wonder how many of these idiots she had to endure and whether she ever had a kind doctor who 'got it'...I know they exist now, as I'm sure they did then. And I'd like to believe that Dr. Dumbass Dictator is the exception to the rule. I've tried the rationalization that maybe he, too, was having a rough day. But nope—still doesn't justify his dumbass-ness as far as I'm concerned. I know that there was some doctor, whether kind and well-intentioned or a cruel bastard or neutral and benign will never be known, who diagnosed Irene. And there were probably hosts of others who treated her that were all somewhere on the scale between wonderful and terrible and flawed and saintly complete with the human foibles that we all carry. It's truly sad that she experienced such worldly unrest that she had to hide herself away from the cars and the people and the noise and go somewhere quiet and green with nurses and doctors in blank, comforting, white uniforms. I hope now she's finally free and in a wild and colorful place where who she is and how she is, is exactly perfect and not a disease but a gift.

It's a mod, mod, mod, mod world

What would the experience of being a mental patient be without the joys of expressing oneself artistically? Art therapy is not just basket weaving anymore. It has a whole new persona, which seems to incorporate the much-ridiculed idea of indulging the inner child. What activity in real 'mainstream' life compares to getting primal and basically regressing to kindergarten with finger paints, glitter glue and crayons? Office supplies just don't cut it—sure you can make a ball of colored rubber bands or decorate your cubicle a bit to reflect your personality but there are certain built-in limitations aren't there? We got an array of materials to work with that would make a craft store jealous. We even got neon colored feathers to intersperse amongst our decoupage boxes and various cardboard creations. Having grown up with a mother who was not only a beauty queen/model but also an interior designer/artist—I was no stranger to the rush that creativity can give one and the seductive powers of its distraction and absorption in something outside us. I became a big fan of Mod Podge (a type of craft glue)—pouring it over everything I created to give things a nice waxy sheen. I wanted to start my own Mod Podge religion where life's ugliness could be made better by simply applying the Mod. I became known as the Mod Podge Queen—a dubious distinction to be sure but I'd been called worse. I made boxes that the other clients admired and imitated calling their recreations a "Courtney" box. I had become known for a certain style—using cartoons from the New Yorker as my main, not-so-secret ingredient. Since I wasn't selling them I didn't worry about lawsuits. But being copied was both flattering and strange. I went into a zone when making these and time became a separate entity that passed at its own will completely unnoticed by me. I even had one woman asking me if she could 'watch' my 'process'...My 'process' consisted of delving in and getting paint and glue everywhere—under my fingertips—up to my elbows, in my hair and all over my clothes. It was therapeutic I must admit. What sucked the joy right out of it was having to explain the 'piece' afterwards...what had inspired you, what you'd been thinking of or 'going for' as far as a message, etc..This was why I would never have lasted a minute at either art school or film school. I had written a few screenplays and done a few paintings for my own amusement. Not that I am averse to feedback when it comes to my writing but when it came to picking apart things that I made for the pure, sheer fun of it—I didn't want to talk about it, or share it or hear about it—I just wanted to do it and be done with it. And move on to something else.

When people ask the question, "*Where do you get your inspiration?*" I seriously want to laugh at them (in an affectionate way—not in a pretentious or obnoxious way at all). I may look at their outfit pointing out that they are wearing certain earrings that picked up the green of their eyes or notice that they're sporting a cool watch or whatever. And I tell them that every time they get dressed they make choices. And that inspiration is nothing more than making a series of interconnected choices—whether conscious or not...And then lots of people rebound with "*Oh...but I'm not creative at all...not a creative bone in my body*"... Funny, that self-taught anatomy lesson didn't seem to stop you when you were five, or seven or even ten imagining whole invisible worlds and telling stories or drawing or making rocket ships out of empty refrigerator boxes or forts out of couch cushions and sheets. I could see people next to me allowing their perfectionism to stop them—I even heard one woman say to the facilitator... "*I can't make anything as good as that so why even bother—what's the point?*" Apples and oranges again. I started feeling almost guilty that my boxes were both a source of inspiration and envy. I mean—they were just freakin' painted boxes made in art therapy for crazy people for God's sake—we were not talking Picasso here!

So I moved on to drawing, which I am terrible at, but I don't really care and the atmosphere seemed to become less competitive again. But it was quite a lesson for me—again the envy card and its destructive nature. The worst was when someone—trying to be facetious said in front of the whole group... *"It's not fair—she's pretty, she's funny, she's nice, she's smart and now she's artistic, too...Don't you have any flaws?"* She thought she was complimenting me and being lighthearted but it made me sick to my stomach and after laughing good-naturedly I told her one of my main flaws was that I smoked and that I needed a cigarette. So, I excused myself and went outside with her words beating in my head. It was like she'd been inadvertently saying *"What's YOUR problem?—the rest of us here have real problems and you should just grow up already!"* It was so powerful to hear the message I'd heard reinforced growing up... *"You have everything going for you so cheer the hell up already!"* So what? So what if I am everything you think you want to be and I'm still not happy? I wanted to scream at the top of my lungs: *'It's not always what it looks like!'* It was hard to realize that the tables had been turned back in my direction. I'd spent the last year and a half envying my sister's happiness instead of sharing it with her because I couldn't take it all in or help comparing my life to hers. Is this what we do as women? Is this how competitive we are that we can't support someone whom we perceive as 'better off'? What a crying shame because we are all missing out.

Art therapy became a playground of sorts for me—with the good aspects of a playground and the less positive features as well. I've learned over time that as much as people want to be put on a pedestal nobody knows what to do when they get there and the old cliché is true; it is damned lonely sometimes. I'm not sitting here saying pity me—I'm so wonderful—or lamenting like that old hair commercial that we could all relate to in one way or another: *"Don't hate me because I'm beautiful."* All I'm saying is that you have your beauty, too—you may just not know it yet or feel safe enough or ready for it to open that painted Pandora's Box.

Kiss Me, Kate

Kate was everything I wasn't. She was a Southerner, a mother, a chain-smoker (my *'if you can't beat 'em join 'em'* smoking seemed like dabbling next to her lifetime three-pack-a-day, full blown habit), and she had come to the hospital full of hope while I'd shown up hopeless. In addition to all of those hats, Kate wore a few others as I'd come to find out. Diagnosed with DID (Dissociative Identity Disorder aka Multiple Personality Disorder), Kate had 'alters' or sub-personalities that would appear when she'd 'switch' or morph into another personality. She counted seven in all but admitted that there could easily be as many as twelve for all she knew. I don't know how many I met in the 4 weeks I knew her. To me—all the many colors and moods made for a vibrantly interesting, nurturing, brilliant and funny woman who touched my heart on a level where fear of the unknown cannot exist. Kate told me witty stories of how she'd 'lose time' and the many embarrassments that this phenomenon had caused for her and her daughter over the years. Her daughter called it 'spacing out'. There were scary moments too, but most of the time she had her disorder under control and only 'switched' in therapy sessions where she felt safe and contained. I had studied spirituality a lot by the time I met her and wondered if she'd considered that she might be channeling? She just looked at me like I was crazier than she was for suggesting such a thought. But she did admit that she was psychically sensitive and picked up on a lot of things before they happened.

Like many sufferers of DID, Kate had endured horrific sexual abuse at the hands of her stepfather when she was a young girl. Her brain fragmented to protect her and what had once been an asset was now a liability and with only 'Sibyl' to refer to, she wanted and needed to know more about up-to-date diagnostic and treatment options. While 'integration' had been a popular goal during early days of diagnosing this illness, it was no longer the norm it seemed. Now it was deemed more appropriate to honor each individual 'voice' as though it had a message to impart and a purpose to fulfill. And in hearing the message and fulfilling the purpose, the theory went that integration would happen naturally—the 'dominant' personality assuming all the qualities of all of the other 'sub personalities'. This was what Kate had been told by her psychiatrist at home, anyway. Her experience in the treatment program where I was enrolled was quite different and actively discouraged 'switching' which was a subject for many cigarette puffing talks and lots of angry venting on her part. Her fluffy blonde curls, wildly gesticulating arms and coke bottle glasses gave the impression of a demented librarian on crack.

Nevertheless, not wanting to judge by appearances, I'd listen and nod my head and make reassuring grunts of assent. But most of the time...I had no idea what the hell she was really on about. But I could identify with the raw fear in her voice, the restless anxiety in the furrowed brow and manic pacing she did. She just wanted to get better...and didn't we all? No matter how many personalities (or in some cases lack thereof) we had, didn't we all yearn to be more balanced, more peaceful in our hearts and minds and less haunted by the demons of the past or imagined tortures waiting in our future? Kate was a generous sort—she'd share her cigarettes and her stories and her laugh easily and often. All delivered with the lilting rhythmic beauty of the slow Southern drawl that belied the rapid-fire zigzagging of her mind's various thoughts. I told her that in a way she reminded me of my grandmother—another spitfire redhead who loved to cause trouble and was encouraging to a fault. I shared with Kate how when I saw pennies I always thought of my Nana with her 'pennies from Heaven' and 'penny on the ground means good luck' expressions. Both Kate and my grandmother were that rare combination of wonderful storyteller and excellent listener. Kate and I shared all sorts of stupid things, me about how whenever I saw the color purple I felt like an 8-year-old girl, or how freezing it was here at night versus where she came from or how wasn't it odd that there were no mirrors in the place—did they think we'd all become narcissistic if we could use something besides the backside reflection of a CD to tweeze our eyebrows? More than likely it was because they were afraid we'd break the glass and use the shards as weaponry. Kate had been prepared and brought a makeup mirror—plastic and purple but broken at the base...She'd joke—*"It's just like me—broken—but it still works—and when you look at it you can see yourself"*...And she was right—looking at Kate I saw myself. I did not see someone who was divided into lots of different people—I saw someone who reflected lots of different qualities--most of them kind and loving. I saw someone whose beauty shined through when her head tilted back and an unexpected deep-throated laugh bellowed out. I saw someone who elbowed you gently but insistently in the ribs when she wanted to make a point. I saw a woman who genuinely was in a great deal of pain, carrying and venting her anger in a steady stream of staff-bashing, but determined to heal at all costs.

"I came here to get better and it's like they want to make me worse." She complained one day. *I'm not just here for me, I'm here for my daughter—I can't stand the pain and fear in her eyes anymore when she looks at me...and now she's trying to raise a family of her own...she doesn't need this. My husband doesn't need this. I don't need this."* She wiped away a tear in frustration with the end of her sleeve. Her desperation was a living thing...it actually pulsated between us. I didn't know what to say. There was nothing to say that would make it all better. This was a problem beyond words, pills, hugs and even beyond compassionate listening. We communicated with silent eyes. I tried to telepathically send her the belief that somehow she could and would and deserved to and needed to get better...even if it was elsewhere. She sent me all of the love of a mother who wants her daughter to know that she's trying her damnedest to heal...to break a cycle of pain.

One day—Kate had had enough of the program's stringent policies and her ever-deepening frustration at not feeling understood or free to be 'herselves' (all of them—even the male ones) so she up and left out of the blue. No note...just a few things piled on my bed to indicate that she'd ever even been there at all. A small fleece throw blanket with moons and stars on it, the plastic purple broken makeup mirror, a pack of cigarettes and a bowl of pennies. It was like my Nana had kissed me on the cheek from the Other Side through Kate's sweet gesture. Maybe she really was channeling after all.

"Toto, We're Not in Kansas, Anymore"

During my hospital stay there were days when I would literally be scratching at the windows. The iron mesh covering was there ostensibly to not only prevent escape but also to keep the glass intact so as not to tempt the 'cutters'. I'd encountered cutting and burning when two years earlier I had worked as a dorm parent in a residential treatment center/high school for troubled kids based in the Berkshires. In charge of a boy's dorm with kids ranging in age from 14 to 21, I realized early on that I was in way over my head. During the orientation week, myself and the other recruits became crisis trained which the school staff insisted we probably would never need as there hadn't been an outbreak of violence in ten years that had necessitated restraining kids in order to keep them safe. For the first six months, I spent the majority of my time finding my feet and bonding with the boys, building trust and getting to know their individual personalities. Things were going along well and I garnered a reputation for being kind, fair and firm and had gradually won the boys' respect with my patience, humor and laid back manner. When I got stressed I would let them know and it would pass quickly. Like the time one of them ran away and I got the 3am phone call to report to the dorm for an emergency meeting with the runaway's dorm members to understand what had happened. While I had one fellow staff member scouring the local streets with a flashlight, I filled out the police report and made it crystal clear to the other kids that if any of them ever pulled a similar stupid stunt they would pay dearly. But overall, I felt I was good at the job and had hit a stride. The boys were always engaging in daily good-natured bickering amongst themselves and would test me from time to time to see how much they could get away with. Which, considering the school's stringent rules wasn't much. So our little domestic world was moving along nicely when I was called into a staff meeting about the girls' dorm across campus—who apparently were having 'lots of trouble'.

'Lots of trouble' turned out to be rioting that would last five days, engaging all of the staff members in rotation to do restraints, to break into a room where the girls had barricaded the doors, smashed out windows, were cutting themselves and writing obscenities in their own blood on the walls. We had girls threatening to swallow broken glass, several 911 calls and at one point I actually took a fellow staff member to the emergency room for a bite wound. Yes—that's right—one of the girls (a seventeen-year-old) had felt the need to sink her teeth into my friend's thigh, both breaking the skin through her jeans and drawing blood. It was after this incident, which followed a stretch of having been in a virtual war zone for almost a week that I took a serious look at my work environment and felt scared. The next few months were a blur of meetings and staff members were quitting left and right. The general consensus was that not only were the kids endangered but the staff's safety was also at risk. The school was under investigation by the state and I increasingly disagreed with the stringent practices some of which seemed arbitrary and designed more to humiliate than educate. Finally, after 8 event-filled months, I quit and left after a friend of mine had quit suddenly and there was a virtual tribunal to discuss his irresponsibility and that we were now to basically consider him a 'runaway' who was to be 'invisible' as in--no contact permitted. This smacked way too much of cult like (and we know I am not exactly a fan of hive mentality, don't we?) behavior to me. Never mind the fact that this same staff member had virtually risked his life on a frequent basis during the riots. He also was the main person called in (due to his bulk and muscles) any other time when violence had erupted in the boys dorm upstairs from where I was, where the less well-behaved kids were. He'd been spit on, had a chair thrown at him, been cut on the arm with a piece of glass and also, in between all these indignities had taught the kids science. To watch the senior staff vilify him was too much for me to bear and I realized that this was no longer a place I felt I wanted to be. I'd ended up there after a series of jobs had failed...or after I had failed...to get into the flow and to follow authority...I'd ended up there by accident it seemed...one day I looked up butterflies...I'd recently gotten my tattoo and felt a deep connection to their transformative symbolism. I'd found this school which was a residential treatment center for kids who were troubled (I could SO relate) & whose mascot was the butterfly to signify the struggles of adolescence. I went and visited the campus and was taken by the beautiful surroundings and impressive mansion that was on the main campus. While my friends were safely ensconced in grad school, law school newly married and having babies...I was running off to save the world from God knows what. Or maybe it was to try and save myself...that's probably the more likely scenario.

So when I was at the hospital, I half expected a repeat of some of my wilder moments at the school but nothing so dramatic ever really happened. None of us were minors so if we ran away or escaped it was usually treated more like someone had basically just signed themselves out against medical advice. During my brief time at the school and even briefer time in the hospital environment I did notice some definite parallels between the two places. While the girls and women seemed to be more likely to suffer from cutting, burning (with razors or a cigarette into their own flesh) purging (vomiting) and deep depressions, the boys and men seemed to have anger issues as well as drug and alcohol addictions. Though after having dealt with the rioting girls who had behaved like rabid animals, I no longer felt that gender stereotyping regarding anger was in the realm of rational thinking for me. These damaged souls sought comfort in each other and puppy love romances sprung up just like at any other high school, as well as forbidden flings between staff members...I gracefully managed to avoid that fate thank, God...seemed like these were intense relationships with that summer camp urgency feel to them...Watching people interact in such a bubble I noticed that mostly women turn anger inward while men are more encouraged to express it outwardly in some physical display whether it be through sports or beating the crap out of each other all in the name of good old fashioned machismo. Women have been known for our cattier and subtler ways of dealing with our rage...but it is never so cut and dried is it? We may not all be doing extreme sports though I'm sure there are plenty of women who do and God Bless 'em...But we have our resources for dealing with anger—cold silences, smashed dishes, shopping and lots of Ben and Jerry's. So when discharged to the women's treatment center I wondered if it would be like my all girl's high school and how the dynamics would unfold. Also, the house was a living experiment in a particular brand of therapy known as DBT— (Dialectical Behavioral Therapy) which to me rather sounded like an obscure chemical or stock exchange symbol of some sort. But I tried very hard to go into it with an open mind. That didn't last too long.

DBT/CBT—The New Religion

Move over Kabbalah, there's a new religion in town and it has more than a red string to counter evil—it has a whole workbook! DBT is a cultish brain reprogramming system called Dialectical Behavioral Therapy and CBT is its less airy-fairy counterpart (Cognitive Behavioral Therapy). Both are fancy versions of 'turn that frown upside down'—but first feel the frown, name the frown, own the frown, understand the source of the frown and then start exercising your smiling muscles...On a good day it is psychobabble, on a bad day it is utter drivel. It may work wonders for Dr. Phil but for the gaggle of social workers administering it in the women's treatment program I was discharged to after lockdown, it was such second nature that they didn't even realize that half of the time they sounded like aliens speaking another language. Don't get me wrong—for the ten years up until my attempt and subsequent hospitalization I had inhaled the self-help aisle, the New Age aisle and the psychology aisle at every bookstore I encountered. So to me, a usually open-minded person when it comes to new theories about shifting gears in thought patterns, to say these paradigms were unhelpful I'm fully aware is a rather bold yet informed statement. I don't just want to sound like some junior high kid who when having trouble with Geometry declares it 'stupid', slamming the textbook closed in a fit of embarrassed frustration.

"I'm going to write my own book." I declared definitively to Jackie one day. *"One that doesn't insult people's intelligence...I'm so tired of people equating crazy with stupid."*

"What will your book be like?" Jackie probed.

"It sure as shit won't be about freakin' bubble baths and drawing fluffy, pink clouds." I retorted angrily.

"Write something real...all anybody in here wants is to read or feel something real... you could totally do it. I'd buy that book in a heartbeat." She encouraged.

Socrates' 'dialectics'--the art of asking questions to answer questions or spark more debate is often a valid and wonderful way to teach and learn...But when you are advising a suicidal person to take a bubble bath or draw a fluffy cloud when they are in crisis it is not only ridiculously insulting—it is downright dangerous. So needless to say—I was the 'challenging' one that dug into the material with zest and turned everything inside out—pointing out flawed or faulty reasoning and questioning everything to the point of being that pain in the ass that every-body wished would just shut up already. Mainly because there were no answers to some of the disturbing questions I raised and my questions were designed to force the Ostrich to shake the sand out of its eyes. Having always been the 'good girl' and rarely challenging authority in a classroom setting (everywhere else but not usually in school) I was rekindling the girl who had come to life in Mrs. D's Religion class my junior and then torturously redundant senior year as well. This girl challenged the woman who called gay women and men *'the flippin' lezzies and homos'* while preaching God's love. This version of me chal-lenged her teacher's narrow-minded midwestern sensibilities and outrageous racist comments about African Americans, Jews, the gay population and basi-cally anyone who wasn't a 'devout' Catholic like herself. Once, I remember my friend had leaned over and asked me a question in an exaggerated Irish whisper *"What the hell is she talking about?"* As I leaned back to answer, I was caught and Mrs. D. asked me to 'pick up my hair'...I gave her a blank stare. She gestured what she wanted me to do and I complied, sweeping my hair back into a ponytail held loosely by my fingertips. She nodded and singsonged, *"I see. So you DO have ears...next time.... USE THEM!"* She was a charmer that one...

Suddenly, while suffering more from agonizing boredom than anything else, in group therapy about Anger Management or Post Traumatic Stress Disorder I became that 17-year-old kid again. And every teacher/group leader was Mrs. D. It was an undoubtedly an unfair way to make my point by unleashing old venom on new unsuspecting victims. I tried always to keep it about the material and never made it personal—on the surface. Underneath, I was reconnecting with the rage of swallowing hundreds of *'because I said so'*s or *'it's about faith'* or any other pat, dismissive answers that are designed to cover the fact that the ask-ee really has no idea but cannot simply admit that. I wanted too much to be right to get much out of this workbook and I felt that disappointment that only the genuinely curious can feel when put off with non-answers. On a scale of 1-10 on the humility scale I was at about a -3. I was liberated from the lifelong yoke of needing desperately to be liked and I was delighting in trying on the 'problem child' role—one that I'd never dared fully explore before. I was allowing myself to be 'negative' and 'difficult' and to roll my eyes outwardly when I thought someone was feeding me BS which was often since I thought the workbook was ill-written, ill-planned and ill-executed in the classroom formats. This was one of the most progressive group-therapy living experiments in the country? Then why did we have a meal-planning group where we busted out ancient, rotting, yellow-paged cookbooks picking recipes and writing elaborate grocery lists? My feeling was that these were life skills classes that if you didn't know by now then you should just pack it in. I wanted emotional survival skills not petty things like which would be better for the chili—red peppers or green?

I know it sounds like I'm whining. The truth is I was a better sport than most—and I was and am not a grumbler by nature. I might make the occasional flying comment that would make everyone laugh and lighten a tense atmosphere. I'm no saint either—if something sucks I'll complain like the rest of them, get it out of my system, and then go on about my business. We had some champion complainers and gossipmongers in the house. Most of the time, I tried to steer clear of the many mini-dramas or personality skirmishes that erupted from time to time. This was when my intuitive ability to read a room, the people in it, the interpersonal dynamics and rising tensions came in handy—and these were often the moments I would pick to sneak away for my clove cigarette breaks outside. I have since given up smoking but I truly believe that at the time it was the perfect excuse to go out and gaze at the stars breathing in the night air and reviewing the scenes of the day. One night I saw some boulders around a tree and placed them carefully in a circle. In the middle I gently placed the pinecone I'd picked up on my walk that still had some sticky sap on the scales. I inhaled deeply to see if any Christmas tree scent lingered...something that would take me outside of this institution with its walls and limitations...back to something earthy and organic. The grass beneath my knees was slightly damp with night dew and I breathed out the horrors and terrors revealed in the discussion groups and breathed in the crisp air. I felt Wiccan and peaceful.

With my pinecone circle I discharged the day's feelings of horror at hearing the rape, beating and incest stories that the other binmates had poured out. With each exhale, I would release other people's pain that I felt I'd absorbed energetically throughout the dayworld wandering from group to group—like smoking it was a rhythmic, meditative breathing sans toxins. I reviewed my CBT and DBT 'skills', taking what I liked and leaving the rest behind. I left a lot behind. What I took with me could fill three journal pages. But I guess that's three more than I had at the beginning of the program and I sincerely learned more from the process than from the actual materials themselves. There were of course one or two staff members I was able to connect with who did help me tremendously. I may not have always liked their methods but they did get through. And who was I to judge? I was praying to a pinecone, fer crissakes.

Tough Love for Wusses

Tough love is a concept whose intrinsic value has often escaped me. Excuse me—but isn't love the antidote to toughness usually? So how can there even be such a thing, really, as 'cruel to be kind'? We've all had more than our share of these 'for your own good' experiences strewn throughout our lives that are supposedly character building. Missing the pop fly that loses the game teaches you humility and how to be a good sport while catching the pop fly that wins the game teaches you self-confidence and introduces you to the taste of victory. Again, this is one of those black and white areas that needs some grey shading and blending for me to fully grasp its utility in shaping one's destiny. If bullies are tough and kindness is associated with the band-aid kiss that will make it all better, then how are we to navigate between the landmines of the harder edges and soft feather touches of the elusive thing called 'love'? I've always suspected that tough love is more about ego involvement than its unconditional counterpart. The self-professed tough love artist gets some sadistic twisted kick out of administering fatal blows and then delivering the line "it's only because I love you and I don't want to see you to get hurt." So kicking me helps this process, how exactly? I knew of a woman who delighted in the retelling of a story which demonstrated how she had taught her 4-year-old boy that the stove was 'hot' and therefore to be respected and treated with the utmost caution. She had held his little finger on the coils for the briefest of moments eliciting a yelp and look of betrayal and mistrust from her son. She always chuckled when recalling the expression on his face. The story both horrified and educated me. It was her flawed yet effective way of trying to control her young son in some important way while protecting him from a much more powerful force of nature that she could never hope to control, really. It was backwards logic...but it made sense in its own way, too. She would rather he get a tiny bubble blister on his finger than set the house on fire with the potential for dire and devastating consequences.

I don't have kids yet but I have nannied and babysat since I was 12-years-old. I have changed more diapers than most of my friends who are now young parents ever will. That thought blows my mind sometimes. Everyone delights in telling me that it's different with your own kids—you'll see. People love to say, *"You'll see..."* don't they? Almost as if they are gleefully yet mostly harmlessly wishing you ill...and at the same time conveying that they are privy to some ancient secret that makes them the member of the long-suffering know-it-all club. Smugly claiming that it's different than you can ever possibly imagine until it happens to you. Funny—I think that could be said of having my wisdom teeth out. I expected it was a routine procedure and something that was a matter of course—everyone does it, right? With four impacted teeth and the subsequent chipmunk cheeks, blood-soaked cotton mouth pads, vomiting from the painkillers and general misery it was so much worse than I could have anticipated. I have since had two or three major surgeries and nothing came close to the horror of the wisdom teeth extraction nightmare. My tattoo was far less painful. So having gone into it with the 'this won't hurt a bit' mentality I was completely unprepared. But as far as other experiences go—I feel that people with their exaggerated claims of how tough/scary things like parenting, sky-diving, or going on a spiritual journey of any kind are doing others a service by over-prepping the novices. This is one of those rare cases where I truly believe tough love works. Parenting is the hardest thing I'll ever do? OK—thanks for the warning. But now, please shut up, and let me get on with trying to meet Mr. Right so I can find out for myself.

While in the hospital after my 'meltdown' (I refuse to say breakdown as I am not a car), I met a nurse who epitomized tough love in the best sense of the term. She consistently stayed on everyone's ass about nutrition and the importance of bipolars having and adhering to a sleep protocol in order to prevent one's bio-rhythms from getting out of whack and adding one more challenge to the already sensitive chemical balancing act. One of her pet peeves was diabetics who didn't watch their insulin religiously. This was enough to warrant a diatribe that could last anywhere from 20 minutes to an hour depending on how grave the offense. She would somehow have an intuitive sense of who was having a particularly hard time emotionally. I remember pacing in circles frantically in my room after a grueling group therapy during which too many details of a woman's incestuous molestation had been revealed and I was so upset that I wanted to tear my own skin off after her vivid descriptions of the years of evil she'd endured. Nurse Tough Love came into my room, listened to me ramble and rant almost incoherently and said gently but firmly *"Your brain is fighting you right now, that's all... and you have choices—you can fight back, which might get you even more wound up, or you can give it a rest...what do you want to do?"* Taken aback by her sensible approach to a near panic attack, I stopped in my tracks and considered her sound advice. I gave it a rest...after some deep breathing and journaling I felt less psychotic and more able to form thoughts that weren't flying at a zillion miles a minute. After this mini-episode one of the doctors told me that I would sometimes experience the downside of being empathic and empathetic—I could very well take on other people's stuff if I didn't work on setting and strengthening boundaries to avoid this all too common trap. Advice that sounded suspiciously like the 'get a thicker skin' comments I'd heard for thirty some odd (some odder than others) years. But maybe it was finally starting to sink in. That night as the moonlight poured in the window with its shining silvery glimmer I was comforted to think that this was the same moon that had been and probably would be around forever. It made me feel small and insignificant. It made my problems seem less urgent. This helped calm my agitation with its 'reality check' perspective. Even though that is the kind of check sure to bounce because reality is always changing. Embracing change, I'd always been a fan of the moon in all of its wondrous stages. Which was ironic now that I was officially *loony*.

The Moon and Me

Lunatic. Loony. Moonstruck. Everyone in the mental health care field knows there is really something to the tossed around phrase: "It must be a full moon..." While most studies have not turned up hard data linking the lunar phase and erratic shifts in human behavior, anecdotal evidence seems to suggest otherwise. For example—my dad put himself through college by working at the State Hospital on the 3rd shift. He is a rational, thinking man—not prone to random flights of fancy whatsoever, (though I have seen him well up at the beauty of a hummingbird) but even he reluctantly admits that the patients (they were still patients back then) became much more restless and agitated as the moon grew fuller. And working third shift he had certainly seen his share of odd behavior. I myself have often noticed an increase in insomnia and racing thoughts coinciding with the waxing, rather than the waning parts of the lunar cycle. Now—when I say I noticed—I mean I noticed after the fact...like a pattern you are mildly aware of but don't follow closely or pay attention to religiously.

When I was younger, I always felt like the moon was a distant, shining friend and often marveled at the old footage shown over and over in movie clips or news tidbits of the first US moonwalk. The moon has had a romantic reputation and soulful tendencies, too, with its nocturnal grace and constant, mercurial shifts. Childhood myths about the man in the moon or about it being made of green cheese only added to its mystery. Once, I had a boyfriend in college and we were having a romantic interlude under the stars when we looked up and noticed there was a perfect ring of light around the moon—like the opposite of a shadow...a luminescent visual echo of sorts. I told him it was good luck... A few days later he looked it up at the school library and found out it had something to do with pollution. We broke up shortly thereafter. But there's no breaking up with the moon—her imagery is everywhere. There's ET riding a bicycle across the moon, pranksters drop trousers and 'moon' each other, George Bailey is depicted in a cartoon by Donna Reed as lassoing the moon; in 'Blue Moon' the sitcom, Maddie and David do the will-they-or-won't-they dance for what seems like forever until they finally do...Moonlit walks, moonlight shining in windows casting an eerie incandescent glow and moonshine, a potent beverage whose mere fumes can knock you off your ass. Teenagers 'moon about' when they experience their first unrequited crush, the cow jumped over the moon, etc.

For an insomniac the moon can be bittersweet. When it's the middle of the night or in the wee hours of the morning, moonlight mocks you and keeps sleep at bay. In the hospital—as I already mentioned, I got a break from the jealous moon when she tried to steal my restful hours and make them restless instead. Sleep meds lulled me into a place that even the moon could not reach. Did I miss my nighttime companion? Sometimes...but sleep was bliss and for that I would forsake my friend—at least for a while. But reunion was inevitable. Like that one friend you know you can't divorce no matter how many fights you have. You may take breaks from each other but you will always yearn for the good parts of the friendship and develop a convenient amnesia (not ECT-induced usually) for the difficulties. The moon kept you awake? Messed with your mood? Admit it--it's still one of the most amazing things you have ever beheld in this lifetime or any other. I think sometimes that if there is such a phenomenon as reincarnation then it's no wonder we have such a visceral reaction to things like the moon. It's a reminder; a guidepost along our journey. When I was little I would wonder if the moon could talk what would it say? *"Good—night, sweet dreams"* or *"Hey—make sure you photograph my good side!"*

Whether you have a special connection to the moon or not it's there in the backdrop of so many of our important collective cultural memories. It's the source of countless songs, stories, romances, mysteries and beauty. It's nature's nightlight and we often don't even notice it and we take it for granted or see it for less than the majesty that it truly embodies. Whether a fingernail sliver or a huge ball of light, in all its phases and magnetic modes—it is a mirror for us. It may sometimes seem imperfect and other times too perfect in its magnificent splendor. It reflects shimmering diamonds on the ocean's surface and flashing glints in a lover's eyes or hair. So am I a lunatic? You betcha. In every lovely sense of the word.

Dream a little dream

Insomnia was the nasty goblin beast that persisted in impeding my healing process and I tried everything I could to kill that little troll-like sonofabitch, believe me. Relaxation CDs, rigorous daily exercise to try and tire myself out, no caffeine after 2pm, reading boring books—some of it worked sometimes but not consistently. The zombie I became was a frightening version of my former self. Hag lady looked back at me from the mirror and I seemed to have aged ten years in just a few months. Functioning becomes a haze of robotic movements for the insomniac. Sleep is an elusive, unrequited lover that is the target of your obsessive fantasies. I couldn't remember what a good night's sleep was or the last time I really caught any Zs…I tried to net those little fuckers with my multitude of tricks but the goblin bastard always intercepted. I have one friend who claims she hasn't slept a full night since she was 14. Nothing majorly traumatic (well—she did change schools at about that time which can be stressful she supposed) had occurred to precede this shift—she just felt like her brain had decided to go haywire and blames it primarily on the true onset of adolescence and the realization that her childhood was officially over. She says she has gotten used to it. I don't know how but she claims that she's made peace with her goblin and even befriended him. According to her, he helped her get through law school with the added study hours. I'm not sure about that but if it works for her then I guess that's fine. I, however, need my sleep. I had come to both love and hate my bed. It was a mocking place of hope—an inviting, warm cottage in the forest with a hungry witch and boiling cauldron inside.

I saw a white peacock once and wondered if it was nature's cruel trick to put this anomalous bird next to it's more colorful counterparts as if to say.."*Yes—you're pretty but you'll never be magnificent…*" It was out of place—just a bit off center. And this is what sleep deprivation does—it skews your vision of the world, drains it of its color and makes everything seem surreal. For months this half-existence had been merely an exaggerated form of wakefulness that wouldn't subside. Or let me clarify—my mind was up and running but the body wanted to be horizontal regardless. So it was war…the winner would only be determined by how long I could lay in bed with eyes closed, brain whizzing and body revved but exhausted. I was on complete overload and each night it got worse. That's when the nightmares kicked it all up a notch...now instead of slipping under to murky dozing dreams I was being chased, smothered, stabbed and each night was like a tragic opera playing under my eyelids with me as the diva every time. Not exactly what most women have in mind when they think of being a diva. In my dreams I was always running from myself and never getting away fast enough. I realized that while you may be able to fool yourself during daylight hours the subconscious lies in wait, maliciously rubbing its hands together and getting ready for the lights to go down. When I told my former therapist about these dreams she suggested that it might be stress. Yeah, ya think?

One night I lay awake, mind spinning and when the night nurse cracked open the door to do 'checks' I asked her if she would talk to me for a minute...I was in a near panic attack and starting rambling at her, embarrassing verbal diarrhea all the way. I wound up with the soap operatic,

"I just don't think I can do this anymore. I can't!"...I sobbed. I was freaking out.

A veteran nurse of probably 500 years, she simply put her bifocals down, looked me dead in the eye and said in her no-nonsense tone,

"Oh yes you can. And you WILL." She just stared at me for a full minute and I dunno what kind of hoodoovoodoo she performed but I began to calm down. It was as though she had hypnotized me...and for a change it actually worked.

I had tried hypnosis before on the 'outside' and that helped a bit for a while until the dreams gradually caught up with me. I remember one recurring nightmare I used to have as a kid. I was in my childhood home and for some reason a circus had been in town and all of the animals escaped. Yes—all of them. From the trumpeting elephant and dancing bear (who was never dancing in MY dreams) to the lions, tigers and even an organ grinder's monkey complete with miniature suit. What can I say? I was a creative kid. Anyway—these beasts just circled my house trying to get in the windows, sitting on the roof and sneaking in through the basement. It sounds implausible now but to an eight-year-old with a vivid imagination it was entirely possible and quite literally my worst nightmare. I remember it down to the smallest detail. The lion's flashing teeth, the tiger's growl, the bear's ungainly paw swiping at the door screen. And the damned monkey cackling the whole time I scurried around the house locking and re-locking doors and windows. The elephant would be much larger than life and under his massive weight the house would sink until there was only dirt to be seen through the curtains and then the fear switched from being torn apart by wild creatures to the suffocating buried alive theme. Either way—it was a lose/lose scenario. Never liked the circus much after these dreams first appeared on the scene.

My grown-up version of these dreams was being chased by someone wishing to do me harm. A nameless, faceless, someone (or thing). Now that I was older and had seen about a billion movies, I had a more sophisticated range of terrifying images to choose from. Fire, drowning, rape, murder, apocalyptic disasters…each dream was a blend of all of them. I started to crave yet fear sleep. Luckily—these dreams lasted only a few months and then something broke…snapped…what was it? Oh yeah—my mind. I think that by the time I turned the key in the ignition and prepared for the ultimate sleep—I was ready for whatever realm lay beyond this one—I believed that nothing could be worse than my nightmares, my day life and the dawns and dusks that I was happy to relinquish for a little emotional peace and quiet. Or so I thought at the time. And I was just so damned tired. Luckily, now I can honestly say that my sleep situation is much tamer…I think the med combo I was finally put on has slowed my nightly adrenalin rushes to a minimum—a side effect I am eternally grateful for. It's a gift to wake up refreshed instead of feeling like you've fought dragons with a toothpick all night long. It's also nice to realize that you don't have to necessarily die to get a little rest.

Bulldozing

If I were to break down my relationships with family and friends I could split it into two eras essentially. There was the pre-attempt me and the post-attempt me. People in my orbit reacted considerably differently to me after the attempt. Eventually this would fade but for a while it was an interesting phenomenon to behold. Lots of "I love yous" and more hugs were the most noticeable difference. It was as though we'd all had a wake-up call and one of the outcomes was an increased expression of affection. The unasked question was "What if?" What if I'd died, what if I hadn't been found, what if they never got the chance to show me how much I meant to them. Some people just got pissed or scared or self-protective and stayed away entirely. But mostly the attempt reminded us all that life is fragile. These new unaccustomed displays of naked emotion were both comforting and unsettling. I had crossed a line. It was clear that people saw me now and instead of thinking *"Oh there's Courtney"* they suddenly felt the urgency of wondering if I'd try again—before they got to show me that I was important to them. I understood this and welcomed it mostly but a part of me resented that it could take something so dramatic to provoke this kind of loving behavior. It is all too common to take others for granted until some outside force threatens to erase them from your life. In my case it was an inside job. I wasn't diagnosed with some terminal illness, I hadn't been in a car crash…yet I had come to the brink of death nonetheless.

This is where the taboo concept of 'attention seeking' comes into play. Had I been attention seeking on some level? If I was, this forced and sometimes seemingly fake or self-serving attention I was now privy to from my loved ones was in a word…weird. I had wanted to be invisible after my early years of being showered with attention and affection. I had felt overprotected and smothered, the pressure of meeting my own high expectations and living up to the ideal image I had built of myself. I felt alone and disconnected. Perhaps I was seeking some sort of sign from the universe that I could be loved and was in fact lovable just the way I was. Not the always-striving-to-be-better, smarter, prettier, thinner, more creative me--the best friend to everyone but herself. But the flawed, imperfect sometimes ill-tempered, sometimes hermit-like in need for solitude yet also craving social interaction me. The me who knew that a lot of what she'd been fed in the guise of moral correctness and appropriate behavior had been a poor substitute for true acceptance. The me who knew that being 'good' isn't always possible…and the me who could just be ok with that. The me who could just be. I knew if I was to not only survive but to really 'live' a full life I had to get to know that me. And I needed an awfully big shovel to sort through the shit that surrounded that me in onion layers. I had helpers who brought their own shit and their own shovels and sometimes we'd excavate together, but mostly we'd just look at the shovels and laugh suddenly realizing that we probably needed bulldozers, really.

I know there's a whole school of thought out there that believes that therapy in general is a waste of time and money and simply about talking to hear yourself talk or reliving your childhood and never moving forward, never letting go of the past. I would say this misconception can be summed up by Socrates' statement (good ol' Socrates again—we like him) *"The unexamined life is not worth living"*…Sure—in this day and age we can't all allow ourselves the 'extravagance' of self-examination…we much prefer to stumble ahead blindly and repeat the same patterns over and over than God forbid actually slow down enough to break unhealthy chains and reconfigure the links into better formations. What of the multitudes of starving children, war torn countries, poverty and violence you might ask? Can they plop themselves on a couch and resolve their survival issues with a little Freud or Jung? No—of course not. But if we as a collective consciousness thought about and talked about our innermost fears—perhaps—just perhaps the blind and grasping greed and unthinking automaton global politics and business would develop—oh I dunno—a conscience maybe? And then some of these problems—rather than just being background noise on the six or eleven o'clock news would seem more like the problems in our own backyard instead of remote happenings unfolding a half a world away. I passionately believe that exploring this interconnectedness and our self-created feelings of separation (common themes in therapy) could actually heal a lot of the world's ills on a grand scale. So that's my argument and defense for why I believe in therapy. To me it's a shame that therapy has become fodder for an arguable or defensible stance. But it is what it is. For some people buying expensive toys can be therapeutic at least temporarily until the novelty wears off and the emptiness inside them sharpens. For others a religious connection to some superior being or higher power fulfills the hole inside them. We all have our different false gods. Food, sex, work, and the arts...these all are wonderful distractions from the fundamental longing and yearning everyone has to discover the meaning of life. The point of it all. In therapy family of origin issues do play a large part in determining where thought patterns came from. So then there is the common criticism that the blame game begins here. Blame is only a small part of a larger process. Acknowledging inadequacies or anger inducing things help a person move forward because instead of skipping over that unpleasantness (which really does lead to dwelling there ultimately—not the other way around) the goal is to make peace with it and see it through a new lens. I know I've made a lot of strides in forgiveness. And I'm not just talking about forgiving others but the hardest thing of all—self-forgiveness. To forgive is not just a religious act. It is freedom. And it isn't ever total or perfect. It's only another part of life. In excavating my childhood I have learned that this piece of the puzzle is just that—only a fragment of a much larger picture.

The Codes of Love

I adore my enigmatic mother yet am often baffled by her unique brand of mixed-message maternal logic. The non-negotiable "*Wear a hat*" in winter rule was always my mother's favorite. She favored berets. Each season with the first significant snowflake I sailed those puppies, felt Frisbees soaring like misfit tropical birds, into the nearest snow bank to be hidden until the springtime thaw. "*Don't take a bath when you have a fever; don't cry it'll only make things worse,*" or to calm a child's nightmares after an ingestion of too much horror movie gore, "*It's not real blood -- it's only ketchup.*"

There is no rhyme or reason to a mother's logic and it can vary from day to day. Growing up she'd often lament that she hadn't bought new clothes in ten years and then at the store would deny herself even the privilege of trying things on saying: "*When I lose ten lbs.*" I always wondered: "Then what will happen? Will everything be magically better? Was it those ten lbs. that made her so angry and sad all the time? Did she hate us and blame us for stealing her youth and beauty-queen looks?

"Artists shouldn't have children," she told me in her studio one day and a look of grief mingled with fury crossed her face so quickly I wondered if I'd imagined it. Was I to be punished forever for the chances she didn't have growing up? The risks and roads not taken? Were the fetters of family life thrust upon her or were they of her own choosing? During her better moments she softens and admits that she wouldn't trade us for a spot at the Louvre for one of her paintings. Other days she'd probably sell us all for a spot at the local credit union. And who can blame her? For years she was overworked and underappreciated like most mothers are.

"I'll make you some soup...it'll be OK". Her tolerance for illness was much higher than her tolerance for 'backtalk'...She is an excellent and compassionate nurse. In high school I faked many sick days just for that nurturing tenderness. Sometimes, I try to catch her, pin her down, and make her look at me...really see me. Like all mothers, she always looks, but never sees. She looks with the painter's critical eye, if it isn't visual, it doesn't exist. She comments on a new hairstyle, shade of lipstick, outfit, colors and shapes. I used to unfairly think that's what her children were to her...colors and shapes and endless needs to be met. I feared we frightened her with our neediness, she became restless, wondering, waiting... *"When's it my turn?"*

"You shouldn't let a boy paw you--he won't respect you", "Don't ever call a boy...he'll lose interest." "Let them come to you." When I was fifteen I'd think—*"Who IS this person? Where did she come from? Does she even know what century she's in?"* I often stepped back, feeling her overprotective, outdated ideas hit like fists. I knew other people who had close relationships with their mothers. One friend I have now is best friends with her mom/pal. They talk about everything. But doesn't she judge you, warn you, criticize, nitpick, and nag? *"Doesn't she make you crazy?"* I'd ask... *"Sure she does. But she's my mother and I love her...we get along pretty well."* I go silent, feeling both shame and envy.

Before the attempt, getting along never came easily for my mother and me.

There've been long stretches of chilly silence between us over the years. With all of her quirks, her aloofness was the hardest to fathom. She claims it is she who was judged and I who was hard. Nevertheless, despite all of our years of misunderstandings, it is more than ketchup that connects us...it is flesh and bone and tears and bitter words and slaps and hugs. We share the same face with only slight alterations. Of all the things my mother ever told me the most bizarre and memorable was this one: *"Don't ever settle for the crumbs!"* I'd been digging in a Doritos bag getting all the salty stuff at the bottom and something in her must've just snapped that day. She crumpled the bag and threw it out the car window... oblivious to our "We don't litter," policy. I cried. I wanted to tell her that the crumbs were the best part. The broken bits at the bottom. Just like in life—those salty broken bits that give life its flavor, its intimacy.

We're both getting older now and working daily towards healing and forgiveness. Now we laugh about her zealous overprotectiveness during the early years and she gently reminds me that I didn't come with a manual, or a translator for that matter...

It sometimes seems like a slow, uphill battle. But we're assembling the crumbs that are not soul-scraps of wisdom passed down from one generation to the next, but the rich and salty bits at the bottom...flavored with years of hardened tears that if shed too soon probably would have only made things worse. These are all the things my mother told me that I never understood...some maternal gibberish that always...always only had one translation: *"I love you, accept my love, receive it. And most of all...Be gentle. For it is a very fragile thing."*

I now know it can take a lifetime or longer to decode these messages of love. And I still don't like berets. But I love her more than any daughter could. The good parts and all the rest, too. It's what makes her human; it's what makes her real. And it makes her more beautiful to me than any tiara-wearing, paintbrush-yielding, Florence Nightingale version of a person who is as deep and complex as the star-strewn night or as colorful and mystical as a sunset over the ocean. Is she still a bit 'difficult' at times? Yes. Would she still like to 'put me through a wall', sometimes? Definitely. But now, most of the time we can laugh about it and move on.

My father, on the other hand, is another mystery to me as I'm sure I am to him. He is a successful, charming, handsome man who draws people like bees to honey. He is the kind of dad who for the most part treats all the women in his life like princesses, yet won't buy himself a sweater without deliberating for a week. His Irish temper would flare occasionally and when it did you better run far and fast to get out of reach. It would take a lot to set him off but when he blew—escape was the only viable option if you wanted to make it to your next birthday intact. We're talking beet-red face and flying spittle angry. These incidents were few and far between though thankfully and mostly his job kept him so busy climbing the ladder to success that he had little energy left over for domestic squabbles. But he did take us on wonderful weekend excursions and day trips and essentially spoiled us rotten. My sister and I are still probably daddy's girls and would rather call him if we were stranded by the side of the highway at 3am than Triple A. Because he always comes through. One of his frequent sentences is *"Do you need any money?"* But apart from material things his loyal love for us is a real and tangible thing. Once I'd been traveling for weeks in Europe, was smelly, dirty, out of money and found myself in the middle of a train station in Milan. I had opened the train schedule which unfolded like a map and was looking at it when bird flew overhead and *splat*--decided to relieve its bowels right on the part I was reading. I lost it completely. Called my dad blubbering and blabbering incoherently that I was sick of this shit (literally) and I was going to miss my connection and my scheduled flight home from Spain and I wanted to come home RIGHT NOW. He, used to these middle-of-the-night meltdown calls from both my sister and me, managed to calm me down and went into his 'problem solving' mode. I should go and get another schedule, wash my face in cold water and he would call to see if we could change my flight—I was to call him later in the day—emphasis on 'day' and see what steps to take. I was at the tail end of my travels—which had been wonderful for the most part but suddenly—my last week in Europe I'd become unbearably homesick and he must've heard it in my voice. Even after a last ditch effort sprint to the airport—I did actually miss my flight and my father donned his superhero cape and came to the rescue, AGAIN, rescheduling my flight for later that same day.

This episode is only one of many that epitomizes that my father is, in fact, the bomb. Between his and my mother's combined strength—I can honestly say that I was raised with love. They were strict and they made mistakes along the way like all parents but they loved intensely (sometimes too intensely I felt) with a fierce longing to keep me safe from life's inevitable cruelties as long as possible. In the end—they couldn't and these past few years have been a long overdue wake-up call for all of us. But like I said before, now—for the most part—we can laugh and move on. Or we can cry and move on. And that—is major progress. Therapy has been a huge part of it. Having a fourth party to intervene and help us decode and defuse old triggers. We may never completely speak the same language. We may never fully get it. But you will never meet a family who tries harder to bridge the gaps and stay with the love.

Lots of love and the ring of truth....

Another thing I inherited from my mother besides good teeth is the ability to furnish a home on a budget. Thanks to her, I am a bargain hunter with unrivalled skills and talents for unearthing unique, funky, artsy and tasteful stuff all at rock bottom prices. Over the years, I have truly been the 'salvage-and-rescue' queen. 'Trash-picker' and 'dumpster-diver' are some less flattering terms for those of us who have mastered the art of so-called shabby chic... 'Thrifty', 'frugal', and 'resourceful' are some other descriptors. It has become so much a part of my life that I cannot...physically cannot...pass a yard sale or flea market without checking out the various and sundry wares...dust and rust are not deterrents in the search for the perfectly weathered antique trunk. I like sleek, contemporary and new things, too. But mixing the old and new together is the best.

Growing up, once or twice a year we would all pile into the pea green station wagon (puke) or later the upgraded canary yellow station wagon (double puke—why did shitboxes always come in bizarre colors adding insult to injury?) to go to this auction that took place every weekend a few towns over. The auctioneer, Betty Salvoni, was a tough but fair woman who sat high up on a bench (not unlike a judge in a courtroom) and quipped dry remarks as each 'lot' of items was brought out and the bidding began. Her austere bun and skunklike streak of white hair against jet black (had the woman never heard of hair dye? Or the Bride of Frankenstein?) she wielded her gavel, microphone and sarcastic wit—always giving a good show along with the JUNK.

"Ok...what do we have up next Teddy?" Teddy stood at bailiff-like attention, always very serious...her straight man. Teddy probably was a retired bailiff come to think of it...He'd yell out the box lot number and my parents would get their ping pong paddle ready, a silent nod of communication between them. Then they'd be off and running...

"Do I hear 20 to start, there are some lovely pieces of china in this lot, Teddy...some without any chips or scratches. I think someone loved these teacups very much and took good care of them, I hear twenty do I have twenty five?"

I would get caught up in the dance, mesmerized, watching my parents have entire wordless conversations... *"Do we need this? Can we afford it? Will it make us happy? Go ahead. We deserve it. Let's wait on that one and see what else comes up next."* All of this was said with the body language that develops between two people who have spent a few decades building a life together on shoestrings and heartstrings. These were not just boxes of someone else's dusty discards to them, these were future memories. These items would live in our home and become part of us. They would be the glue that held us from paycheck to paycheck as sacrifices were made to pay for braces and private school tuition and the ever-frivolous light bill.

It would not be unusual to go home with a box of bric-a-brac of completely unrelated items—Chinese yo-yo's, mixed with old sheet music and several pieces of mismatched flatware. But every now and then my interior designer mother found a treasure. And my sister and I endured with squirmy impatience. We were torn about whether to whine or behave because maybe something really good would come up as the auctioneer's glasses slid further and further down the bridge of her nose. Sometimes there would be still-in- the-package toys amidst the dustier items and once a really cool (well—really cool to an eight-year-old anyway) strawberry-shaped lamp popped up that I begged and pleaded my mother to keep bidding for. The auction house was a wonderful, mysterious place with a thick smell of mustiness and the heavenly aroma of the greasy cheeseburgers that the place sold gave off.

We loved the idea of buying something that someone else had owned and thought that each item had its own story. What was new to us had once been someone else's NEW purchase, had lived in their home and seen decades and in the rare case, centuries come and go.

It's a great metaphor for life, too—this blending of the old and new. You may some days wish you could scrap your entire life and start from scratch…new job, new house, new car, new wardrobe, new body, new romantic partner…hell—even new kids on those particularly challenging days when the little cherubs are pissing you off. But what's better than the comforting gaze or smile of an old friend who knows you inside/out and loves you in spite of your embarrassing 5th grade talent show performance of the Charleston to Prince's 'Little Red Corvette'?…(don't ask, thank the gods that Keith Karlson was out sick that day). At some point, though it pains me to admit it, thrift shops do start to lose their fun appeal and just become a hassle and quite frankly…a bit smelly. They are a great resource for those less fortunate for whom donated second-hand goods are not about style but about necessity. They are fine for acquiring the occasional knick-knack or interesting conversation piece but really…beyond the college years they have to be used less and less and then eventually comes the day when you realize it's time for *gulp* 'grown up' furniture. No longer will castoffs cut it—ugly plaid polyester sofas must cede to leather loveseats with clean lines that come with their own special care kit. Ratty, moth-eaten sweaters will be replaced by at least one item of cashmere (even if you have to save half a paycheck to afford it). You start to be less 'shabby funky' and more 'streamlined funky'…

This does not just mean conforming and becoming an automaton with no personal sense of style. But again—after hearing my dad quip that after my mother and I dragged him to a famous chain discount store he 'needed a shower'…one does start to see old things in a new light. And I'm not talking antiques which have their own level and cache in the furniture realm—they have dignity and value. I'm just talking—old. Not 'vintage' or 'retro'....just sad and wilted. Not 'gently used' or 'needs TLC'...just fodder for the junkyard. Some things have many incarnations and go through transformations (like the chair that my mother has reupholstered 7 times—that chair is like a member of the family by now)...But other things were meant to be more...disposable. Just like certain personality traits...not the good ones, of course...But the people-pleasing thing for example—needs rehabbing. Just as things hold certain energy so do out-dated and worn ways of interacting with the world. Being nice for niceness' sake is not the same as being kind, compassionate or empathetic out of a kindred understanding of another person's plight. I'm not advocating rudeness but I am saying that at some point this former Catholic schoolgirl decided to trade in the plaid pleats for something a touch more daring. And I have never regretted it or looked back. Now—I'm more likely to wear bohemian chic tops mingled with more updated styles, or just the old classics, t-shirts and jeans....And my style reflects *me*...artsy, quirky, serious, playful...whatever the mood and fancy strikes me and feels comfortable.

Whether you prefer the solidity of the known or the novelty of the latest gadgets, your own brand of style inevitably evolves over time. Your tastes change, your temperament ripens into its fullness. 'Weirdness' becomes 'eccentricity' and 'unfocused' becomes 'eclectic'. There is a certain flow to acquiring and releasing things. It's a cycle that requires constant minor adjustments and readjustments. When acquiring there is always the guilty pleasure of contemplating the purchase one feels pretty clear that they could ride that high exactly two minutes until the dreaded buyer's remorse or sticker shock set in...And the risk has desire, temptation and satisfaction all built into one transaction. Oh, there's always rationalization of course...the 'need' for something that will brighten up a room—that corner really needs a plant or something. However, does said plant 'need' to park its ass on a $350 plant stand?? Different story entirely. Same with a personality trait...I really need a change—I feel so stagnant with my life...does not necessarily have to translate to "I need to hop the nearest plane to Italy or France or Thailand or—fill in the blank exotic locale..." Feeling bored does often lead to impulsivity. Impulsivity is one of my least favorite words these days since it is one of the traits (and I mean listed in the psychiatric bible and everything) of Bipolar Illness. So yes—while the majority of you can make 'impulse purchases' for the bipolar person it is defined as a dangerous pathos. We are not often the best credit risks.

At the treatment center, stories circulated about notorious buying sprees that almost everybody there had succumbed to at one point or another. One wealthy woman had spent $150,000 over the course of 2 days. That's three lifetimes' worth of Betty Salvoni's eclectic auctions! We wondered why she was in there with the lowly masses instead of having some lackey dig up Freud himself who would simultaneously fan her and feed her grapes while he psychoanalyzed her.

I remember my first impulse buy when I was fourteen—the year I discovered the dangerous combination of jewelry and layaway. Jewelry I had known about since my jangling, gold-bangle-laden grandmother had given me my first amethyst ring at the tender age of five. But layaway was a new concept that according to my fiscally conservative parents would be my certain undoing. I set out to prove them wrong. This little episode involved lots of tears and door-slamming—your typical teenaged dramatics. At the time—my parents were so angry you would have thought I had murdered a litter of kittens instead of fallen hopelessly in love with an aquamarine sitting prettily upon a thin band of gold, flanked by two tiny diamonds. I loved that ring with the intensity that only a 14-year-old can muster. I saved my babysitting money and the cash from my after school job.I visited that ring like it was a cherished relative on their deathbed. When the layaway period was over, I bought the ring, silently flaunting triumphantly that I had, in fact, been able to make my 90-day deadline. That ring shone like a beacon of accomplishment and teenaged rebellion. I think for my father it was a beacon of another kind. A beacon of his financially irresponsible daughter carving out a long road ahead of her. But over the years we have all been able to roll our eyes good naturedly over the infamous 'ring episode'....In college I pawned the ring for pizza and beer money. I know what you're thinking...but truly by that time it had served its purpose well. And I was starting to learn the reason that "creditors" rhymes with "predators"...Coincidence? I think not.

Compulsive shopping is listed as an actual symptomatic behavior associated with Bipolar Disorder. The afflicted have been known to go on sprees that devastate their savings and incur huge amounts of debt all in a weekend high. Manic episodes aside, shopping has been a therapeutic experience for the most part for me. Whether I shopped 'til I dropped or grew in some new small way I've found little moments of truth in the marketplaces where lies are often sold. I was smart enough to usually see through the sales pitch and then brave enough to overlook that in order to obtain that perfect, most glorious, amazing had-to-have-it thing. Each thing, person, relationship spoke to me like it/they knew my inner soul or the future home it/they would be adopted into and inhabit...I've acquired and shed places, people, ways of being that no longer worked. I've held onto the meaningful friendships and family ties that have been a part of my early history. All of these were pieces of me and built new layers around the core of who I really am always stretching into who I want to become. Each lot that presents itself in my life may be filled with the treasures and the junk, but also with love. Things can only be a weak reflection or expression of who we are. And when who we appear to be changes as a constant (as it does for even the most steady sort), then we must reach out and grasp something to cling to. To ground us, to keep us from the 'crazy' whims that whisper every day.

'What's in a Name?'

There are two expressions I've always hated with equal passion: *"Grow up"* and *"Settle down"*—they never equaled good news. When parents tell a small child, as they are wont to do in moments of total frustration, "Oh, grow up!" or the other, ever popular, "Just settle down!"—they are creating a paradoxical image in a small child's brain that these directives are necessary in the human development process, but at the same time oddly anger provoking. And they are often linked in this way—growing up becomes synonymous with settling down into a prefabricated reality, trading in lofty dreams for attainable ones, seeking comfort over thrills. Yet there persists that part of us that resists—maybe it goes dormant for awhile and then resurfaces as a midlife crisis. Or maybe the Peter Pan syndrome prevails and we end up bouncing in and out of jobs and relationships trying on and discarding them at whim. Or maybe it's even genetic...

At some point in one's life the concept of ancestry exerts a pull that must be explored. Recently, I have found myself pondering my "Walsh-ness" and wondering why the Walsh family crest is a swan with a sword piercing through its heart (ain't that grand?) and our motto in Latin translates to: "*Wounded but not dead.*" How freakishly appropriate. This implies that we resurrect from our sorrows and rise again into the light, refreshed and renewed from life's struggles or piercing disappointments.

We may be pierced by the world's sharpest edges but we are resilient of mind, heart and spirit. I can identify with this in the simple fact that my life (thus far) has brought me challenges that I've met and conquered—even the ones that almost conquered me. I've also learned that you must play to your strengths and learn from, but not dwell on, your defeats. I'm a self-admitted defeat dweller sometimes...when it's productive, to stay in the moment until the lesson is learned and revisit it from time to time as a gentle reminder. From my mother I have inherited the artistic flair and the 'pretty' face she's always wanting me to adorn with more makeup. I get my height and thickness of hair from my dad, as well as my ability to charm and make goofy puns and even his scary temper from time to time myself. From my grandmother I received my boundless curiosity for adventure in the form of traveling and trying new things. I attribute my compassion for the underdog and bouts of quiet introspection to my grandfather's gentling spirit. These gifts were handed down and blended like a genetic smoothie into yours truly. We're all pretty much mixed-up versions of the traits of those relatives from the generations before us.

My mother's maiden name(s) have a place in this, too. A blend of "Libby" (lighthouse Mainers and DAR folks) and Robery, which we believe to be English somehow but are not entirely sure it's not some sort of Ellis Island bastardization of a much longer, difficult to pronounce counterpart. Sorry, mom. But since both my grandparents on my mother's side were dead before I was born—I tend to identify a bit more with the relatives I knew growing up. The ones who are survivors, teachers, people-pleasers, avid learners and incurable smartasses to the nth degree. Yup—pretty much sums us up in the proverbial nutshell. And yes...speaking of nutshells there were a few probable depressives and bipolars along the way. But that's not the point. The point is—well what is the point? The point of the sword in the breast while the neck flaps backwards? This crest really has to be seen to be believed. When I first saw it I took it as a sign of utter doom, that as a family, surely we were cursed. But the swan—now there's a powerful creature. And the whole mating-for-life scenario? Yup, that's us for sure as proven by members of my clan who have gone on to celebrate their 40th, 50th etc. anniversaries. I am continually amazed at the endurance, love and sheer staying power that bonds these marriages together. Not that it's all a party or a picnic, mind you. It truly is damned hard work. But so is wiggling a sword out of your chest without bleeding out.

When I was younger my parents always sent me out the door with one of two departure phrases... *"Be careful"*...and *"Have fun!"*...Usually it was my mother saying the former with furrowed brow and my dad casually tossing off the latter...Over the years they would sometimes switch roles but the words and their meaning were clear. It was the approach to life we embodied. That there was fun out there to be had but you had to be careful how and who you had it with. Choose carefully who you open that big ol' pierce-able heart to and have some laughs along the way. Don't take your wounds so seriously because they generally won't kill you. Watch out for the sword-wielders and keep your eyes and mind open all at the same time. It was a confusing message of love and fear. I never really understood what the priority was—enjoying life or fearing it...because to me the cautious approach often sucked the joy right out of it. Mom, dad—close your eyes.

Let it be made clear here that I am all for safe sex and that's not where I'm going with this... It wasn't just life's accidents or pains or worries that gave us all this 'waiting for the other shoe to drop' tentativeness. It wasn't just strictness or protectiveness or nervousness. It was more than fear, even more than love. It was simply habit. It was a thought-pattern ingrained so deeply over time that even now when something good happens it's hard to just allow that feeling of joy to overtake you without doing the mental Pros and Cons list first. 'Concerns' was another (and still is truth be told) of my least favorite words of all time. As in: *"We just have some concerns..."* Yes—it's normal, all parents worry yadda, yadda etc. But it's always nicer to hear—*"We are so happy for your happiness"* instead of *"We just want you to be happy"*...

And when this unlikely response is the *first* reaction to joyous news that will be the day I know that chocolate will be raining from the sky next and to turn my open mouth of shock up to the heavens to start enjoying the sweet precipitation. I love my parents from the edges of the galaxy and back again...several times over...they are they most beautiful swans I know—inside and out. But swans can be tough...which brings us back to the concept of tough love's ability to strengthen your inner core and teach you the important lessons of humility, temperance and proceeding with caution when warranted. But I hope my lesson to them has been that it's more than ok to occasionally just get swept up in the oceanic bliss that sparkles back from your child's eyes when they are truly happy. And to let that be what it is before letting worry immediately swoop in and dampen it or overshadow it. We're still working on this one both individually and as a family—and they are troopers who are open to soul growth. After all...the sword may sting and leave a gaping hole in your heart—but then you get to choose how to fill up the space and you keep choosing. And there's no right or wrong way to get or keep an open heart.

The 'Real', Real World

One of the disillusionment factors that contributed to my depression was friends and family members' persistent belief that there is a 'real world' and that we should and must really all strive to be a part of this mature and shiny place. However, in a world filled with slickly edited reality TV shows springing up left and right it is becoming increasingly more difficult to distinguish reality from fantasy. Frodo is more believable than primetime TV, and the Ring itself more fathomable than what people are willing to consume on Fear Factor. When I was growing up, the catchphrase the "Real World" meant one in which you paid your bills, showed up on time for work and waited in bank lines (before the advent of ATMs of course). Now it conjures pretty, post-pubescent fame-hungry creatures yelling at each other in a cushily furnished house over who is the most politically correct of all....To be truthful, I always was suspicious of that phrase that would put 'real' and 'world' in the same sentence to begin with, thinking that it was just an inadequate explanation of why all the adults around me seemed to be so miserable.

Back in college, I nannied for a film professor at Harvard and a former student of his worked for MTV in California. One day out of the blue he asked me, ME if I'd like to be involved in a regional casting call for the Real World London. Ummm....will ice cream start raining from heaven next because clearly you CANNOT BE FREAKIN' SERIOUS?! *Yes, please.* I accepted. It was a whirlwind, the day of the event I worked with three cameramen, was interviewed by two local TV stations, and I was the girl with the clipboard behind the velvet ropes.

"What makes you think we should pick you for this show?"

"Because I have two penises and because I ROCK?!

"Thanks—um...we'll be in touch....NEXT!"

We were supposed to keep the interviews moving since there were over 2000 applicants who showed up at the mall--each hoping for their shot at the infamous fifteen minutes we are all programmed to desire that is apparently subliminally embedded in the commercials between cartoons (they get us young), well, that and to whine our mothers to death to buy sugared cereals. There was nothing real about the casting process. We were supposed to look for attractive, interesting people with strong personality types who had some other reason to go to London besides wanting to be on TV, so like maybe they were also aspiring models, singers, dancers or actors....you know....regular joes and janes with perfect teeth. I had grown up watching "Fame" I knew the drill.

Over the years, watching my parents (and hearing about friends' parents) squabble over bills, drag their reluctant asses out of bed groaning on Monday mornings (now knowing it was a labor of love I'll always be grateful for)— at the time I always wished that they were, I don't know...happier or something. But happiness wasn't a concept that fit into the so-called 'real world' paradigm. *"Sacrifice is noble...Struggle is rewarded. Life has its ups and downs—Disappointment is a luxury you can't afford."* These were the beliefs I was being taught by the words but other lessons by the actions of those around me. The lessons were subtle but the vibe was palpable. There was a restless yearning for joy beneath deadened aspirations. An idealist philosophy with cynical undertones. Do your best to make the world a better place...but don't dare to get your hopes up that it actually will be.

I've been called lots of names...dreamer, idealist, New Age Pollyanna, slacker, spoiled (as though I am rotting fruit for having attended private school) and my favorite of all—SELFISH. These are names I learned to call myself along the way, too, even when I was working one more babysitting job, or sweeping another café floor or stocking shelves in the dusty backroom of a bookstore or changing the millionth diaper of a child who was not my own, or doing endless hours of mindless data entry...It was never enough to wash away the original sin of wanting more joy in all its forms—whether that joy be moments of stolen solitude, the satisfaction of a well-turned phrase or an exotic vacation. My restlessness to somehow measure up to an unattainable societal standard of being a 'good girl', 'good student', 'good daughter', 'good friend' was energy wasted on some invisible treadmill with audible whispers urging me to take on more and more until 'burnout' became a way of life that seemed admirable; and words like 'stress' and 'exhaustion' and the hidden game of subterfuge—*"My life sucks/is harder/fraught with more challenges than yours"* were worn like badges of honor. It was a cyclical, seasonal pattern that was unrelenting...running and running from myself and from the opinions of others. It wasn't too long ago that I learned that I couldn't ever be 'good' enough but I could be authentic. Where were my fifteen minutes? Oh but I wanted so much more than that. And I didn't even have one penis, let alone two....but I definitely ROCKED!

Seriously, though, I'm not a starving beggar in a third world country. What right do I have to complain when I have always had a dry roof, warm bed and overfilled belly? This is America after all. Land of the free, home of the brave and all that jazz. What right do I have to whine that it's not enough—*"I WANT TO BE HAPPY, TOO! I want at least 12 and a half minutes if not my full fifteen that I was promised."* Like a toddler throwing a temper tantrum because he/she feels nobody is listening to him/her. Or a silver-spooner used to always getting their own way (we shall not name names since claustrophobia is like a serious problem, too ok?)...

We all know it ain't written in the Bible, or the Koran or the Torah and even the Declaration of Independence only promises the *'pursuit'* of happiness—not necessarily promoting the attainment...Is happiness a human right or a divine one? This was something I'd often ponder when locked up and away from the rest of the world. Mostly the inner voice I'd hear (not to be confused with 'hearing voices') reassured me that it was ok to want to be happy—it was and is perfectly 'normal'. Hell, it was the sanest thing I knew.

One thing I learned was that when that voice speaks loudly in me then I *must* listen. What right does anyone have to tell me, or you or anyone otherwise? If I strive for joy—why does that threaten people who have complacently given up and learned to live bitterly and resentfully (claiming contentment all the while grumbling about their lacks) without it. They live their lives grudgingly accepting that that's just the way it is/has to be/always has been/always will be? That's REALITY. If I yearn for meaning, why does that warrant a knowing laugh from those who believe meaning is derived from the numbers in your bank account, or shiny trophies on a shelf rather than the amount of times you laugh heartily in a day? I'll tell you this—I will *not* be a martyr who allows her dreams to crash on the shore of other people's unfulfilled expectations and wash up like so much flotsam—broken bits of glass and entangled seaweed--brackish buds bursting. Give me the simple flower of wishing any day over that. I grumble and moan and vent and complain sometimes, too—then I do laundry and cook and phone friends. I have learned to let life lift me out of my own head—it's the only way I know to peace.

There are too many out there willing to settle for the status quo—never taking risks and calling those of us who do both 'irresponsible' and 'impulsive'. I try to forgive them their insecurities even as they mirror my own. What if they're right? I ask myself when I can't sleep...What if my whole life is a sham? By whose standards? By the standards of corporate America? Slick advertising companies? Men in robes and pointy hats? Tall buildings able to be leapt in a single bound by non-existent superheroes filled with cubicle-dwelling worker bees? Or by standards of kindness to self and others? By treating one another with respect, compassion and not judging another's choices? By holding the hand of a sick friend while he or she cries or even dies?

I do not think it smacks of entitlement to believe you deserve joy. I believe it smacks of enlightenment. I am not there yet. I will not be sitting under any Bodhi trees or getting nailed to any cross to attain that bliss that comes from self-knowledge. I cannot walk on water but I can walk in a 'real world' of my own making. One that questions inanities born of fear, recalibrates constantly and is open to changes—good, bad, exhilarating and terrifying. I know that sadness is a part of life. I am not advocating feigning it isn't or pushing through it with stiff upper lip, sucking it up, keeping one's chin up or any of that other cliched and unhelpful false 'up' stuff people ignorantly tell someone in the throes and lows of pain or darkness. I don't suggest to get stuck or wallow there either like a pig in mud (though it seems to make the pig happy, anyway)...I believe that there is a way to acknowledge, honor, feel, and release sadness or negativity. I believe that everyone does this differently with their own individual methods and time-tables. I do not believe in telling someone to snap out of their dream and leave the Matrix behind. It's not my job to administer cold doses of harsh reality—the world will do that enough with its many flavors of tough love. However, that said, I also do not believe in candy-coating things either...I have always believed it's important to stand by your convictions even if you don't like the outcome—and you usually won't. So many people are afraid of their own shadowy dimensions that they'd rather skim the surface of life like water beetles. Never delving be-neath to see the beauty of a shaft of sunlight cutting through greeny deeps, stir-ring up silt to watch it dance and settle, rearranging into something new again and again. For isn't that what each moment is? A kind of making-it-up-as-you-go-along, yet benefiting from the wisdom of those who've gone before? Paying homage with each breath to ancestors and pioneers alike. Visionaries, poets, painters, musicians, scientists, seers, kings, queens, oracles, shamans and other mystics who've given us glimpses of the Great Beyond. That's real. That's the world. It's all around you in statues, paintings, songs, even on the ticker tape of the Stock Exchange and in the microchip of your cellphone.

What about 'regular' people you think? We aren't all poets...some of us have to attend to the mundane things of life and have no time for poetry. There can be poetry in the mundane and mundanity in the poem. But that doesn't make any of it any less mysteriously beautiful—and yet—it's also nothing special or out of the ordinary; even though we like to convince ourselves that it is so we can mimic awe. So we can pretend to be inspired by something outside ourselves. Free will gives us the choice to see the world, warts and all, with eyes of wonder and grace or with eyes that are cold and jaded, hiding behind realism as an excuse not to even attempt to reach a higher spiritual potential that sparks in each of us. To be the lazy creatures we accuse others of being who shy away from the hamster wheel of progress. When that same progress makes an 8 year-old pathologized and medicated for over-exuberance? When what were formerly known as garden-variety problems have become full-blown disorders and syndromes, emerging treatment for which includes an army of pills every color of the rainbow. Which reality is real? Which world is this? One carefully edited with contrived scenarios and sound bytes manufactured to create a certain effect? Or something else—a higher order of delicious chaos that swirls around us--refusing to be labeled, slapped in a can and sold on a supermarket shelf? One where if you don't fit into an acceptable category or demographic then you fall down the rabbit hole never to return again. You are for all intents and purposes, dismissed, marginalized, demonized, victimized or worse, deified, held up on a pedestal and then knocked off it just as quickly by the fickle masses. You become crazy and the craziness seems the only true sanity you've ever known.

When the world as you know it has been dismantled by those who are either unconsciously or intentionally striving to keep you in your place, those whom to your face will encourage and seem supportive but behind your back will hold another opinion, that is when it makes sense—is a survival mechanism even, to question your reality. If they are undermining you to others with backbiting gossip then radical reassessment needs to happen. What role are they playing in the demise of your dreams? Or the undoing of your hopes? They have been called 'toxic' or 'energy vampires' in the pop psychology books. 'Two-faced' is another harsh but, at times, accurate description. But according to Zen teachings we should strive to let our perceived enemy become our friend and teach us the hard lessons about ourselves because that is where true growth can happen. In looking at the buttons that are being pushed you hear the ugliest voices of your mind amplified and the boogeymen of needing acceptance at all costs breathing under beds and in closets. So create a new world, one in which you stand up to those 'voices' and hear them for what they are—the whispers of scared children who are testing the bounds of your love. Kids are always asking *"Will you still love me if..."* questions. Friends and lovers are no different—just taller versions of these scared kids, really. The real question is how much do you tolerate and when do you cut your losses and let it go? If it hurts more than it helps it's time to let go. If it's an anomaly or a bump in the road then you keep trying to reach common ground. It's difficult to know the difference. Scabs and scars become bridges to understanding one another better. When you feel your character, your very essence has been deeply misunderstood or attacked then you need to step back and breathe. Is it your ego that has sustained this wound or your spirit? No mere words or actions of another can harm you unless you are in conspiracy with them to allow it to be so. Just like Eleanor Roosevelt said about nobody making you feel inferior without your consent. The problem is so many of us feel so inferior to begin with that any small injury cuts to the core of us sometimes. They may sting and bite, itch and burn....but ultimately you cannot be erased. We really don't begin or end and there is no real middle either. Stay with me...I know it all sounds very New Age philosophical but think about it for a minute. Your world is still real and solid and revolving beneath you even when it feels like jello. Is this just lazy sound bite psychobabble or truth? More unfavorable labels and judgments...It can be exhausting holding them up—and so sweetly refreshing to put them down and walk away. The liberation lies in believing that none of it matters except you, your mirror and your conscience.

But we as a species are interdependent, trusting creatures and it is never that simple. We all rely on each other to reflect back the deepest parts of ourselves, the parts we don't admit to anyone—the glorious and the hideous. The crazy and the ugly. The joyous and the fearful.

Let he who is among you without sin cast the first stone...Let she who is among you without secret desires to be happier cast the first stone. Let all who pretend to be someone they are not and put on their game face every day while their hearts and spirits are breaking cast the first stone...What? Not even a pebble? Well, then. Real world schmeel world--Welcome to crazyville—here's your first official passport stamp.

Coming Back from the Almost Dead

Oh Blah Dee Oh Blah Dah

If I learned anything from this suicide attempt, besides the fact that most automobiles nowadays have catalytic converters prohibiting carbon monoxide poisoning from happening at a rapid rate…it was about new beginnings. And that only when you are tired of waiting for your life to begin are you at your true starting point. After I eventually pushed past the danger zone and started gradually by degrees to regain the will to live, a good friend of mine was diagnosed with Stage IV colon cancer at the age of 32.

Apparently it was pretty advanced by the time they caught it since they don't routinely do colonoscopies for people under 50. Being an elementary schoolteacher who traveled to exotic locales for her summer vacations, for a long time she thought she'd picked up a parasite in South America and that this was the source of her chronic intestinal problems. She figured it was just something that would work itself out eventually, but was a nuisance in the meantime. She would go and have tests and more tests…but it kept getting missed until they found a tumor the size of a grapefruit and eventually decided they needed to operate to remove four of the six feet of her colon but that it might already be too late, the cancer might already have spread.

The horror of discovering her grim diagnosis was a huge slap in the face wake-up call and I felt horrendously guilty all over again. Now—whenever a flitter of a flutter of a suicidal shadowy inkling sneaks in, I think of her. She was and is my catalyst. And she was and is my converter. Her terrifying situation and bravery renewed in me the fact that suicide was no longer an option. Ever. Her tremendous fighting spirit converted the despair in me into an uneasy gratitude that I didn't have to endure the physical agony and somehow my mental anguish paled in comparison to her endless surgery, chemo, tests, tests and more tests. While I'd had my brain picked, zapped, poked and prodded—M. had her body cut open, dissected and poisoned. Our paths were parallel only in the strangest of ways—I had wanted desperately to die and failed. She wanted desperately to live and was failing that, too.

Both of us had felt helpless but my situation improved while hers worsened. I'd heard of a priest who was purported to have healing powers—over her Christmas visit from California back to her nearby hometown in New England, I wanted to take her to this Mass. Even though I'd left the Church years ago you can't turn your nose up at a miracle no matter what collar, skirt, robe or toga it wears. I picked my beautiful eyebrow-less friend up and we took off into the blizzarding night to see this man with the so-called magical hands. She entertained me with a story about her seatmate on the plane from California. Apparently this woman had chewed her ear off the entire flight about her impending divorce, how her husband was cheating on her etc., etc. barely taking a breath and certainly not letting M. get a word in edgewise. M. said that the whole time the woman was nattering on and on she wanted to point to her nearly invisible eyebrows or tear out a clump of her hair (literally) and show it to the woman screaming… *"Hello???! I have CANCER*—SHUT UP!" But of course my friend was far too nice to do such a thing and just suffered the woman's monologue nodding and mm-hmm-ing in the right places. While this story had me in stitches on the way to the church it reminded me of where we were going and why. I felt so helpless but determined that if this guy had an ounce of miracle in him we were bottling some up and taking it away with us.

M. was raised without religion and had an intellectual and secular understanding of the different faiths and so was unprepared for the Catholic knee-torturing stand/sit/kneel repetitions that are practically an aerobic workout. Plus there was the recitation of the rosary (which even I, with all my years of Catholic school, still don't really know except that it's a whole lot of Hail Marys and Our Fathers and some in between stuff—Joyful Mysteries? Sorrowful Mysteries? Which was in store for us?)…

When the priest in question came out we were instantly worried since he looked like he could use a little healing himself. He mumbled incoherently and then after an hour and a half walked around and touched people on the head for a few seconds each. Now—being a 'healing touch' proponent I was hopeful that M.

would get some benefit from this as I've seen some amazing shifts for people (and experienced them myself) with Reiki. But that's a whole other book. She didn't feel anything. I felt a little woozy when he walked by but I'm highly suggestible. After he left and was whisked back to the room behind the altar—I dragged her back there with me for an 'extra' blessing. The father gestured for her to sit down next to him and started murmuring something asking her if she had an acupuncturist...My friend came all the way from California to the East Coast to have a New England priest ask her if she had an acupuncturist???!!! Wonder what the Vatican's stance on that one is? I was glad he spent a few minutes with her even if she could barely understand him she got to have some face time and I think that made her feel a little better.

We walked out into the cold air where our breath lingered in little clouds. I kept apologizing to her and worried that it had been a letdown but she seemed fine about the whole thing and shared how since she was diagnosed she was now just opening up to as many channels for healing as possible.

"*Being Catholic sure is tough on the knees.*" She shared thoughtfully. She looked so tired and discouraged that my heart ached for her. It felt like it was being squeezed dry of hope as I watched her shoulders slump and her head lean back on the car's seat.

I could tell that we'd both been looking and hoping for the miracle but came away with something a bit more mundane. We did have a wicked giggling session in the car about how the singers and guitar player looked like they were straight out of a Christopher Guest film.

"*I felt so bad because I kept feeling the giggles coming on and I had to pretend to cough a few times to cover it up.*" M. confessed.

"*Congratulations....now you're officially an honorary Catholic and you have the stifled guilt and bruised knees to prove it.*" I teased her.

We both just looked at each other and said in unison, "*Acupuncture???!!!*" and we laughed so hard we thought we'd never stop.

The snow was coming down heavily and Christmas was just a few days away.

There was that sense of hope and possibility in the air as each perfect snowflake spiraled in geometric beauty around us. M.'s condition had been getting worse and worse and her most recent report was that she was in uncontrollable agony and that her nausea was causing her to lose more and more weight. It broke my heart but strengthened my resolve. I will live because she can't. I will fight the good fight long after her fight has ended. At that point we were still hoping for the miracle. For the Joyful Mystery. For the rapturous news that her scan would say that she'd gone into remission. Even though all of the odds were against her. We started to worry when her T-cells were shitty but you can't live in a constant state of crisis for any extended period of time. Nobody can sustain that kind of fear long-term. Even when you are dying life goes on. It goes on in you and around you and whatever silvery thread binds you to earth may get weaker and may snap, but while the heart beats and the body draws breath it loves, it weeps, it laughs and it hopes. It hopes for more hope. Hope can be tremendously cruel but sometimes it is the only thing keeping us alive in the end anyway. Death is always the unspoken catalyst to life...we live so that we won't die. It isn't wishing, or yearning, or desire that keeps us alive—otherwise I'd be gone and M. would be getting stronger by the sheer force of her tremendous will.

Six months after the Christmas acupuncture advice mass, I went and visited her when she came home again—this time for treatment and perhaps indefinitely. She'd left her teaching duties and apartment in California behind. She'd been in a pain clinic in Chicago where nothing they'd tried had worked and her nausea was causing more and more rapid weight loss and bouts of dehydration. This time—a cruel trick had occurred. Her eyebrows had come back in full force—a la Brooke Shields so that she was plucking them incessantly to keep from getting uni-brow. Some kind of hormonal thing from the chemo I think. The plucking distracted her from her bodily pain. Little pinpricks caused by tweezers were better than unrelenting agonizing spasms that could last for hours or even days. She was doped up to the gills and slurred like a drunkard. She was even delusional. She'd ordered her mother from the room a few days earlier and her paranoia grew by leaps and bounds. She gestured as though she were holding something saying non sequiturs like, *"I have a cup here with garlic and tonsils, any takers?"* She waved wildly trying to ward off the road signs and aquarium in her way. Her mother's favorite nonsensical statement was made when they'd been in a hotel in Chicago (where they went to check out a special pain clinic) and M. saw the suppositories on the bedside table and muttered, *"You can use anything as a suppository really, fish...cheese...anything."* Conjured up quite a visual. When she told us she was *'not afraid of aardvarks'*, the hospice nurse in the room said that this was a punchline to an old joke. M. was fighting her demons on all levels. Physical, mental, spiritual and emotional. She had a set of crystal rosary beads hanging by her bed from a pilgrimage to a Brazilian healer. She was wasting away but her sense of fight and humor was still strong. One day when she was examining her split ends closely for about a half an hour and her hair shot out in all directions with a severe case of bedhead, I asked her if she wanted to brush it. She just smirked and wryly deadpanned, *"What are you suggesting?"*

After I'd made my attempt, my loved ones kept asking how I could do that to them and didn't I know that I'd be killing pieces of them, too? I didn't think of my soul as being so connected to theirs in such a tangible way. But M. reminded me of the truth of this bond of love. I know that if the miracle turns out to have been having had her in my life however briefly—I will accept that and be devastated to let her go but I'll know that she opened a place in me that was closed before. And if that's what love can do—I think to myself—then why isn't that stronger than cancer? Naive, I know. Sometimes whether we want it to or not—life blunders on. And other times no matter how badly we want it to—it doesn't. You never know what shape things will take and you can't try and mold any outcomes because that defies the very nature of a miracle. M. herself was a miracle. So am I. So are you. Yes you are—and Oprah thinks so, too. Wink.

Sweet Bitterness

I always wondered why the expression was that something was 'bittersweet' rather than the other way around. Seems to me that bitterness often trumps sweetness and leaves its acrid aftertaste burning the tongue and mind. This lesson was driven home when I lay furious, disappointed and humiliated in the emergency room with an oxygen mask's tubing up my nostrils while hospital attendants floated in and out of my consciousness. This was that surreal purgatory time when I felt neither alive nor dead. It was sweetbitter. Everyone kept telling me how 'lucky' I was. They clearly didn't get it. That's like someone who finds out that their husband has left them for a younger woman and some schmo tells her she's lucky to find out what he's like now rather than later…Where is the logic in this? Or when you break your foot and someone tells you you're lucky it wasn't the whole leg—aren't you on crutches either way? This insistent look at the so-called 'bright side' can be an annoying Stepford-esque false optimism that misses its target completely sometimes. Because when you are experiencing life like Job you don't want some idiot telling you how 'lucky' you are that your wife turned into a pillar of salt and not black pepper—think of all that sneezing! I'm all for making lemonade but sometimes you just have to be able to acknowledge that the lemons are sour before you can even begin to add the right amount of sugar. Yes—relatively speaking, most of us are lucky technically speaking. But the Pollyanna approach to life is one dimensional and empty if its sole purpose is to make you feel guilty that you aren't exhibiting gratitude 24/7. While gratitude is an admirable goal to work toward, it is not something you can feel at say, the moment the guy in traffic cuts you off—unless you are of angelic most high-like caliber—this is going to piss you off. And it *should* to some extent because that jerk just endangered your life. In that scenario he's the lucky one…lucky I am a pacifist who does not believe in carrying a gun.

What is luck anyway? Some ascribe it to timing being 'right' as in right time/ right place sort of thing… Others feel that they were born under either a lucky or an unlucky star and are therefore either blessed or ill-fated their entire lives. Charmed or doomed however, we've all experienced bouts of good luck and stretches of bad luck. Learning to ride the wave is what growing up is all about. The Peter Pan syndrome of avoiding the crests and crashes but rather staying just above it all is a tempting trap to fall into. Puer Aeturnus (Eternal Child)… swashbuckling adventures—fighting pirates, flying and having all of your basic needs met with a little wishing and fairy dust doesn't sound so bad after all. But I still remember the sensation of quiet freedom and satisfying independence of the first meal I ever cooked in my very own kitchen...Having lived with family and then roommates for years, when I finally moved into my own place the first meal I ever cooked was 'barefoot spaghetti'...nothing fancy—just an ordinary pasta dish with a little improvisation on the ingredients. Barely unpacked, I roamed around the kitchen while the floor was still drying from its much needed scrub down and rummaging through my newly contact-papered shelves I felt what Peter Pan never experienced—the simple pleasures of adulthood. May have taken me longer than most to get there, (my therapist would gently remind me that it's not a race) but that just meant I cherished it all the more. At the moment I forked in my first bite of barefoot spaghetti—I knew I was 'home'. Right time, right place.

While fortune, fame and lasting romance have eluded me thus far, I've been pretty lucky in the friendship department for the most part. I still maintain connections with pals I had when I was 6 years old. A few high school and college holdovers remain and some from the work world with whom I've bonded through jobs from hell. Then there are my 'New Age' friends who are into crystals, Eastern modalities and energy work. There are others who've fallen by the wayside over the years...There are the psycho ex-roommates from hell who launched into shrill diatribes over cotton balls, the dysfunction magnets and the gay boyfriend who was probably secretly stealing my lipstick. But even these folks meant something to me deeply once—until the inevitable 'break-up' happens where you can't put enough distance between you and the other party and the memories are soured by bitter pettiness and imagined offenses blown ridiculously out of proportion. Everybody who's ever passed through your life teaches you something—even if it's just about who you don't want to become—about the many shades of vulnerable we all share and about how when the honeymoon is over—it's really and truly over sometimes. Pre-attempt I often agonized about these break-ups feeling that somehow, somewhere my people-pleasing skills had failed me. But post-attempt I realize that some people are unplease-able anyway. And that the disease-to-please is insidiously soul-sucking, too. Now if someone is all huffy and gives me the 'how dare you be less than perfect?' crap--I am much more inclined to shed a few tears (rather than sob incessantly or lose sleep) and then shrug it off. I learn from my mistakes and move on.

I can honestly safely say that the ones I feel lucky to have in my life feel the same about me, too. And the rest? Let them wallow in their bitterness while I savor my sweetness...And some days it'll be reversed—they'll taste life's sweetness while I am swallowing the bitter pill. Call it karma, or life's rhythm or justice or luck—it's the taste buds of the heart and mind that experience all of the flavors of love, hate, sorrow, and joy. Sometimes it's blind luck and other times you are merely reaping the harvest of what you've sown (good or bad). Surrender to the ebb and flow...And remember that dark chocolate is bittersweet and who can complain about that?

There's a Madness to my Method

A few times at the treatment center I'd get on a cleaning kick that could last for hours. I rearranged the meager furniture I had (bed and dresser) in elaborate configurations One girl had postered her wall so it looked like any other college dorm room. She was eighteen and had had her meltdown crisis as a freshman on her university campus where she heard voices that were telling her to switch her major so many times that the Dean finally sat her down and asked what was going on. She seemed to be experiencing more than the usual indecision and angst that the other freshmen were and was something else going on? She broke down in tears in his office, her parents were notified and she was swept away to the beautiful hospital grounds that mimicked her own campus but with a few slight and obvious differences. Art therapy replaced Renaissance Studies and Anger Management was the new Psych 101.

"So there are three anger styles primarily...and while we all have overlap most of usually fall into one category more than others." The rumpled social worker with his tie askew and salt and pepper hair mussed, used his marker on the whiteboard to teach us how to be pissed off and how to express it in a healthy, productive manner. Our eyes glazed over immediately. Why does everything divide neatly into threes I wondered? Maybe our brains couldn't take more than three facts at a

time or something. I had thought it was nine. But nine was divisible by three—so maybe the brain broke things into chunks of three for a reason. Or maybe not. I'd ask but he seems really wrapped up in what he's saying...might interrupt his squinty-eyed flow, his deep furrowed brow concentration. I was better off talking to the TV...it didn't judge or look at you like you were being a pain for asking a question.

J. and I became friends one night while watching TV. She was tickled that I talked back to the TV newscasters. She said I was fun to watch the news with and that you couldn't say that about everyone. One week I had nightmares and flashbacks of my attempt and had difficulty sleeping. As the bags under my eyes increased and as I sleep-walked through the day I wondered if it was time to switch meds again. J. asked me if I'd had any 'tricks' I'd used in the past when insomnia became a problem. I told her that at home I'd listen to my relaxation CDs and sometimes that helped. Apparently I'd said the magic words. The next day I had my very own sleepytime CD that she'd burned to help me drift off. It was so sweet and it worked, too!

But perhaps the coolest thing J. did during her stay was to set up a coffeehouse evening. She put up signs and streamers, had a sign-up sheet and everyone participated as though it was a real open mic at a real coffeehouse. She was so cute about it we couldn't let her down. She played guitar and made up a little ditty about everyone at the center, including staff members and she had us all giggling like schoolkids. My talent was to read the back of a tea box. With overly dramatic flair I read the syrupy copy adding my wisecrack commentary and had everyone laughing at my goofy performance. That night we all were unaware of our surroundings in the clinical sense and it was just like a grown-up version of show and tell. When we went to sleep that night the house crackled with hope. It was one of the first times I felt like I was home while I stayed there. The accommodations may have been ascetic, the food may have been bland sometimes but in the afterglow of a night of laughing so hard your face hurts, music, poetry and games—we were all one somehow. I slept well that night I remember.

Another time at J.'s insistence we all had a little 'field trip' to a local parade. I just remember all of us sort of blinking like moles in sunlight at the sensory stimulation and surreal and sudden understated grandeur of it all. There were crowds and cotton candy and marching bands and we clung to each other in the midst of all this chaos. I'd been to hundreds of parades before as I'm sure my companions had, too. But we all agreed later in the car that this one held a more vivid shape for us because of where we'd left and where we were all returning to. I kept expecting one of us (maybe even me) to have a panic attack or get separated from the others. But we appointed a meeting place as a contingency plan and some of us hit the local boutiques, some sat in a coffee shop watching the parade and the others grabbed a front row seat on the curb to feel the whoosh of the passersby and to better smell the signature scent of horse dung mingled with popcorn and hot dogs.

J. was our parade mistress who organized everyone keeping track of the time and meeting place checkpoints. Though the youngest of us all—she led the group with her natural ability to gather us all together and keep us moving. I kept telling her she should become an event planner but she'd brush me off, shyly embarrassed at any compliments. She had on her brightly tie-dyed T-shirt, jeans and Birkenstocks and was easy to find in the crowd which helped, too. She came from a large family and it showed. Though she fell somewhere in the middle in the birth order she clearly was used to caring for the younger ones in her family. She had youth's ability to adopt new families wherever she went. So we were her new charges and she took it upon herself to watch out for us. It was touching and amusing both at the same time. It was also a clever subconscious plan because then the turnaround was that when she was feeling blue, she suddenly had plenty of surrogate mothers, aunts and big sisters to choose from. With bent ear and wet shoulder, I listened to her stories of how college wasn't the right place for her and she'd like to try acting or music maybe but wasn't sure and her family wouldn't approve, etc. The ironic thing was—she had come from a family of creative types. Teachers, musicians and even a prize-winning poet uncle. But her parents, who had always encouraged her and her siblings to learn all about the Arts, showed a conservative streak when it came down to one of them choosing that life. Perhaps it was a case of do as I say, or a protective instinct that kicked in and prohibited her from following her dreams in her own way. They wanted her to develop a penchant for the sciences instead. She was heartbroken and confused by the mixed messages she was receiving. So the voices started manifesting the arguments in her head about which path she should choose and why. It became overwhelming and began to interfere with her schoolwork and even her friends became leery of her.

I think that's why she liked it when I talked back to the TV and answered un-asked questions. When I told Dubya that he was a soul-sucking dunceboy and asked the smirking entertainment reporter if tragedy always dressed in sequins? It made her feel more 'normal' somehow. She, like me, was considered bright and articulate and filled with potential. She, like me, wanted to travel and see the world and absorbed my country-hopping tales with greedy glee. One day, when listening to the war stories of some of the older women; she broke down into unexpected tears (her usual demeanor was sunny and upbeat) and we all asked her what had triggered her outburst. She managed to convey that, no offense, but she was still young enough to cling to shreds of optimism and our cynical views depressed her. She didn't want to become like us (just like I feared becoming like my Great Aunt Irene). We quickly gathered around her, clucking and soothing her, stroking her hair and back and letting her be eighteen and scared, finally relinquishing her 'capable' overly mature role and letting the vulnerability crack through. We reassured her that everyone has their own path and different times of difficulty and tried to put the spin on it that she was clever enough to get her midlife crisis out of the way early. Dunno if she bought it or not but it seemed to take her mounting hysteria down a few notches before it could escalate into a full blown 'episode' and I'm not talking Seinfeld. I'd had one myself about a week earlier where I simply stopped halfway up the stairs, curled up and just put my head down and cried helplessly. The reality of my life had hit me hard that afternoon as I was walking up to my room where I'd been sleeping (in between the night terrors) for about three months and it weighed me down--literally. Two of the other women came and comforted me, brought me tea and one girl brought her laptop with a DVD of some anime thing that she promised would help me shift my mood and take my mind off of my own troubles. They got me up to my room into bed and tucked me in as though I were a woeful toddler post temper-tantrum. And then they did the kindest thing of all—they left me alone. The women in the house had an uncanny ability to sense when you needed ice cream, a foot rub, a song, or time away from everyone. We all helped each other in these little ways. Many times some women bitched about each other in whispery gossip sessions too—they were not saints after all. But we as a 'community' always rose to the occasion whenever someone's gut-wrenching tears melted our hearts and the nurturing instincts kicked in.

It was a methodical and efficient form of kindness and it went on a rotation—whoever was having a particularly rough day--the laser beam of mama-love went to them. We could all switch roles depending on who was suffering the aftereffects of an intense therapy session, hormonal fluctuations, a fight with a family member—all were fodder to fuel our needs and the alpha lionesses fiercely protected the rest of the pride until they needed the protection themselves. You'd only need to overhear… *"So-and-so's not doing well."* and it was like a code that put us all into the selfless gear thinking of tiny ways to cheer that person up. It reminded me of the groups of women friends I'd had growing up. First in elementary school, then at the all-girls' private junior high/high school, my friends in college, and beyond. Men would come and go but the sisterhoods were always sacred and sanity-preserving. Being in a 'group home' for women was no different. We all rallied around the weakest link and helped nurse their broken wing until they could fly again. It wasn't just the milk of humankindness flowing either—it was hard-wired and hard-won. We'd all been there and done that. Maybe men bonded with sports, cars, women or war—cliché—yes—stereotype—yes—true? Absolutely. Caregiving may not be a natural part of every woman—surely there are exceptions just like there are softer, more sensitive men—metrosexuals—exhibit A. But I've seen it in action enough times to know that there is something to it. It kept us sane in our madness. It was a form of support we were used to, so it also had the comfort of the familiar. And most importantly, it reminded us that we were not alone.

The Gang's All Here

Roberta, or 'Bobby' was a fellow 'inmate' in the women's program where I saw many personalities come and go but a few stuck out and will remain emblazoned in my memory. Bobby was about as different from me as it got. Here I was—middle class white girl, Catholic School survivor, straight (but not narrow) and the only things we really had in common were being in emotional crisis and speaking Spanish. I got to practice my language skills and learn some Puerto Rican cooking and Bobby got to enjoy flirting with me while I blushed and reminded her that thanks, but as far as I was concerned she was missing some vital 'equipment' in that dept. After a few uncomfortable initial encounters where I tried to delicately get my point across and she tried to steamroll over it with her 'don't knock it until you try it' logic, we settled into an easy friendship having established some pretty clear, though unspoken, boundaries. I was comfortable with her thinking I was just an uptight white girl and she felt fine about me changing the subject from Angelina's juicy, sweet lips by asking her for recipe tips or inquiring about her daughter. We regaled each other with tales from our pasts and she clearly had it rougher growing up (not that it was a contest even though there were moments it felt that way—"I'm sicker than you" was a weird subtext at the program sometimes and I always refused to play finding it unproductive and victim-oriented thinking—I was there to get stronger—not take pride in how downtrodden I was or why—I felt compassion but wasn't going to make a playground game out of pain).

Bobby had been a member of a girl gang in her teens, had been molested by her brother as a child and was in the process of a divorce from her philandering husband. When I asked her about why she had married a man if she had "always liked girls" as she claimed, she just shrugged and raised a brow ironically as if to say—"That's life..." Like Kate, Bobby had been diagnosed with DID and had several alters—one of whom was a little boy of about 5. 'He' was mischievous and had a playful streak when she 'switched' to his personality. Either Roberta was an Academy Award winning actress contender or she was truly afflicted by this horrible illness of fragmented torture. When she became this little guy her body language, facial expressions and voice all reflected that of a post toddler who was eager to have a water fight, a race up the stairs or sing nursery rhyme songs. Now—I'll be honest…at first this totally freaked me out and when I would chat about it later with her it was like filling in a drunk on what had happened during their blackout. She had absolutely no memory of these times and it was another common symptom that those suffering from DID lose large chunks of time which is scary and disorienting to say the least.

When she 'came to' she would often have a migraine-like headache and have to go and lie down for a few hours. It was disconcerting at first when I didn't know who she might 'be' at any given moment. At one point, she was in a particularly rough patch crisis-wise and for about a week kept 'switching' so much that the staff exhibited visible concern. One day her bed was empty and we wondered if she had taken off as she was always threatening to do. Apparently she'd been brought back to the lockdown area of the hospital because (we were told) she 'needed another level of care'. We all knew what that meant. Another level of security, another level of containment and another level of hell. I saw so many people go into the locked ward and come back worse. They would feign being better for the doctors and Mental Health Specialists but to the rest of us would admit that they were mostly faking so they could gain back some level of freedom. Plus—if nothing else the boredom of the psych ward could get under your skin creating that trapped sensation of feeling like a goldfish circling around and around but never going anywhere.

Bobby often talked about her 'girls'—the former gang members who 'had her back'. It sounded like a sorority with switchblades. Having gone to an all-female junior high and high school I was just about all set with that much estrogen after six years' worth. At times, the women's program reminded me of what it was like to be around so many menstrually synched-up, catty yet nurturing, bitchy yet supportive women. Quite an environment in which to heal. Powerful and difficult, uplifting, inspiring, fun and also a grand pain in the ass. The intuitive powers of women are irrefutable. The psychic powers of 'crazy' women are also quite unique. It's like they/we are tapped into another plane where time can flow back and forth and precognitive dreams, visions, and little 'knowings' are commonplace. Not to mention the fact that we were all on mind-altering drugs to boot. I think that Bobby had a bit of this spooky sense of timing and I know that I got a little tingling feeling every time the phone was about to ring and eerily and uncannily I was always right—it was like a subtle energy crackle and I could have reached for the phone at a few points and picked it up before the first ring. This phenomenon did not continue after I left so I attribute it in part to being around so many other 'sensitive' women whose combined presence packed some kind of kinetic punch. Let's face it...a few hundred years ago we were all the types to have been burned at the stake anyway so in a 'safe' environment where anything went...we mostly just considered these things 'normal'—which is ironic on so many levels.

We were our own 'gang' with hidden rules and complicated codes of behavior. For example—we all did a weekly shopping trip to the local grocery store to stock up for the week. Armed with lists in hand—we'd spread out exhibiting an almost military-like efficiency and purchased enough food to last twenty women for seven days. Now, one would not think this was rocket science. However, each and every week for the five months I resided there (yes—I was one of the old-timers and often teased about how I had probably founded the program I'd been there so long) it was a recipe (pun intended) for disaster. Invariably bread or milk or some rather important and obvious staple would get missed only to create a need for subsequent later mini-trips. It was on one of these mini-trips that I had what we in the program would euphemistically call 'a moment'. My moment consisted of a sudden rage that overtook me that here we were—twenty some odd women (and yes—some were more odd than others admittedly) most with college degrees could consistently forget the goddamned milk AGAIN. With all of the cereal and coffee consumption that we were doing on a regular basis this seemed like a simple enough task. So I flipped out. I had let it roll off my back for several weeks in a row. I got to the point where I just felt that buying a freakin' cow would be a better use of our time and resources...sadly I was voted down on that one. I didn't say a word to register my protest—when we got out to the parking lot I emptied the groceries with the others into the back of the van and then volunteered to return the cart. I did something I'd never really done before in public (fights with family members don't count here). I caused a scene. I took the cart and ran it at full speed towards the carriage holder and **SLAMMED** it into another carriage. It felt so good I **SLAMMED** it again. By this time—I was the crazy person slamming the cart so one more **SLAM** for good luck and I had begun laughing at myself. The other shoppers and my fellow house-mates in the parking lot were looking at me as though they feared for their lives which was so absurd it only made me giggle all the more. Now I was officially the 'hysterical' crazy person who was acting completely off the wall. It was a very satisfying experience because I allowed myself to **ACT CRAZY.** It was one thing to **BE** crazy but quite another to **ACT** crazy. It was my own little rebellion against the lethargy that develops and the easy way one's individuality is swallowed in any kind of group situation where freedom is limited. That noise of the gathering momentum of spinning wheels and metal against metal made me suddenly catch a glimpse of why people like monster truck conventions. Or to watch a building get demo-ed. It had a certain appeal that was undeniable. While suicide is a quiet, private, solitary and desperate act of insanity—(unless you are talking about suicide bombers and I'm not even going there) it does not hold the same **BANG** as two carts crashing. Doesn't even hold a candle to it. So the next time you feel desperate call the Samaritans. And if that doesn't work—get off the bridge, put down the razor, flush the pills and head to your nearest grocery store parking lot. You may get arrested for disturbing the peace but you will gain an inner peace that will make suicide seem laughable. And it's a hell of a lot more satisfying than drawing a bubble bath or a fluffy pink cloud I can assure you.

I'm not suggesting that taking out your aggressions via grocery cart crash therapy or hitting your spouse with soft wands or screaming into a pillow are going to cure all that ails you. But it's a pretty good start. It's liberating in a way that you can't even begin to imagine. I think half of the world's sorrow comes from trying to keep feelings compartmentalized, neat and tidy. Sometimes shaking up the status quo is not only the healthy thing to do—it's the necessary and sanity-saving thing to do in order to avoid exploding into billions of tiny fragmented pieces and then trying to pick them all up and put them back together again like some demented Humpty Dumpty-esque puzzle.

Bottling things up

Apart from the *Towanda!!* moment, I did have another sort of 'incident' that involved a glass bottle, a white van and lots and lots of yelling. One night on our nightly walk I was fuming about something or other—probably going by a friend's 'dorm' and realizing that I couldn't just 'pop in' for a casual visit because I was being shuffled along in my invisible orange jumpsuit with the rest of the chain gang and was in a 'privilege restricted' phase of my vacation at Club Med. We had stopped by the cafeteria and unbeknownst to the group facilitator I had bought a glass bottle of iced tea—which I didn't even think about. It was a violation of the rules since we weren't allowed to have glass. This is an important part of the story and you'll see why in a moment. All of a sudden, almost out of the blue, as we neared the building to return to our stark hospital existence I went into an altered state that can only be described as 'blind rage'. I vaguely remember shouting that I couldn't do this anymore that human beings weren't supposed to be caged, what was our crime—being sick? Why were we locked up and essentially punished for circumstances beyond our control—this was cruel and unusual punishment, etc. I remember the others looking at me and dragging on their cigarettes with curiosity and something even approaching admiration. As the facilitator stepped towards me I told her to back off or I'd smash my ice tea bottle into a thousand pieces on the ground. Security was called. I hadn't meant to make a violent threat—just to have a few more minutes in the open air before returning to a state of sad imprisonment. I felt the injustice of it all and privately compared myself to protesters who chained themselves to things to save trees or something.

But as the white van pulled up, I started to see the gravity of the situation. What if I was taken away somewhere worse—someplace without Oreos? Wasn't this everyone's living nightmare? Being taken away by men in white coats (or in this case a white van)? I strengthened my resolve and yet calmed down when they asked me if I was going to give them any trouble (the equivalent to asking if I would 'go quietly'). I considered my options. I didn't have too many really. So I got in the van and asked where they were taking me. Back to the ward was the answer. I suddenly began to see the humor and absurdity in this now that I knew

I wasn't being hauled off to the Big House. They were literally driving me about a hundred feet and I arrived only a few moments before the rest of the group. Now I was just embarrassed that my little cathartic moment had been so anticlimactic. But when we got up to the floor everyone huddled around me telling me how brave I was and that I'd voiced exactly what they felt, too. A couple of them made bad "don't bottle things up" jokes, reminders to recycle, etc. and we all laughed about it. But that night I realized something amazing. I had gotten angry—I mean 8 on the Richter Scale pissed and the world had not ended. I had been 'bad' and 'thrown a fit' but was almost immediately forgiven. This was so new to me that I was stunned for the next few days.

In my house growing up there were two ways to express anger. Explosively or with extended passive-aggressive chilly silences. And often one would follow the other. Clearly over the years I had adapted a lovely style that blended the two aforementioned ways when dealing with anything from mild annoyance to full on guns out, shootout at noon, rage. There was and still is sometimes a palpable phobia of the less sunny emotions in my family. We are people who are good at a multitude of things—anger is not one of them. My friend across the street had a mother who chased her around with a shoe, a spatula—anything she could get her hands on, really. My parents' weapon was disappointment. Which as far as I'm concerned is far worse than any walloping for the damage to the psyche factor. Luckily, my sister and I were mostly good kids so that our punishments took the form of missing sleepovers or birthday parties, or maybe even the occasional concert. Missing out on these things to an 11, 13, 15, 17-year-old can reach life-or-death proportions though and once I ran away and hid on a hill about a mile away sobbing my guts out, hating my parents, convinced that I must've been switched at birth and even though I was the spitting image of my mother there must be some reasonable explanation for that. Police were called and it was not pretty for the next few weeks. Not pretty at all.

This is all normal adolescent angst, though, right? One would think so anyway. But these offenses set the scene for nothing but heartbreak all around. Because of that little red spark that could ignite us all into flames at any given moment. Anger's power to obliterate and destroy was almost baffling to my friends who thought that there may have been a teensy bit of overreacting on the part of the Mr. And Mrs. of the house. According to most of them—you got mad, you yelled, it blew over. Of course they sided with me and felt my pain. But friends are loyal that way and I loved them for it. But I had to take some responsibility here, too. I may've been 'just a kid' but boy did I know which buttons to push and which strings to pull. This—I was very good at. Machiavelli had nothing on me in this department...so for the most part I got what I probably deserved. But not always. I guess I got tired of trying to be so 'good' and 'nice' that some acting out was to be expected, was healthy even. But this was a few decades before Oprah and Dr. Phil. A few decades before it became unacceptable to smack your kid around in anger and then pretend it never happened later. It was a time when family loyalty meant not saying anything bad about your home dynamics in public and just letting them eat away at you and erode your self-confidence with each passing year. After all—everyone was dysfunctional so why should we be any different? And if you misbehaved you had to be taught a lesson...period. I have worked a lot on forgiveness in this area. I have tried again and again to verbalize the darker moments to hold them up to the light and finally set the boogeyman free. Therapy has helped. Confronting my parents has helped. The fact that they have been open to listening and put pride (or shame) aside and see it from another angle has helped. I've been accused of dwelling on the bad stuff. In therapy I've come to realize that it's totally natural to 'dwell on the bad stuff' until you can bring light to it and release it over time. Not all parties can do this or delve in as deeply as others and that's as it should be. For them—I am the one now overreacting. The shoe is on the other foot it would seem and as we all muddle though together I remember the childhood that brought me here. I remember both the good, the bad and all of the in-between. But you don't have to make peace with the good stuff do you? Maybe it's about finding a common ground where you can all level the playing field and feel a bit more equal in the power distribution. Instead of a struggle maybe it can become a series of negotiations. And it doesn't have to be taboo to remember. It doesn't have to be something that stays in the shadows. And losing your cool doesn't have to kill you. And saying 'I'm sorry' isn't an automatic end or eraser to the pain in the past—but it's a solid beginning to a better future. And you can let the air out of the bottle sometimes...and it can be ok. You can let some things go, let others blow over or let still others blow up. But punishing yourself for it later, or forever, does nobody any good.

Confessions of a Former Flower Child

Growing up in the 70s and 80s in a small but diverse suburban neighborhood was an early education in intercultural relations and respect. My sister and I thought nothing of the fact that across the street were a Chinese American family, next door to them was a family from India and down the street an African American family. And a few streets away were Serb-Croatians (then known as Yugoslavians). It was a wonderful environment that combined with my grandmother's early encouragement would plant the travel bug seeds that later came to fruition. During the 80s when the song *"We are the world, we are the children, we are the ones who make a better way..."* came out we could all relate. We were the world, we were the children and we were trying to make the world a little bit better in our own individual and collective ways. But I don't mean to make us out as the mini-UN...We had our squabbles and disagreements just like any other neighbors. There were scraps and misunderstandings over dogs marking their territory on cat-owners' lawns, an unthinking kid picked a prized flower before it's time (yup—that would be me and I can tell you--serious drama ensued), teens raced late at night without regard for laws of gravity, speed or noise pollution. I remember going to the different houses and inhaling the exotic cooking smells of each. I remember how the neighborhood mothers all screamed our names at dinnertime (the lungs on these women!) I remember the lemonade stands and Haunted Houses in basements and make-your-own-pizza and/or bowling birthday parties and catching leaves in the Autumn as they swirled and danced in the wind downward into our greedy little fists only to be crumpled into leaf dust.

It truly was pretty much a happy childhood. I never went to bed hungry. I was never in fear of my life or cold or without shelter or wondering if I'd make it through the night as bombs exploded near my head. It was safe. It had its moments of sorrow and weirdness—like the child molester who lived down the street and had been preying on little kids calling himself "Uncle Charlie". Charlie had a basement full of kiddie lures—pinball machines, jars of candy and storybooks. My friends Tracey, Amy and I all went to see Charlie's lair one day since we'd heard rumors that he had a veritable carnival in his house and gave away bags of pennies and free candy. Ages 10, 11 and 12 respectively we knew Charlie was 'odd' and we even knew the whole 'don't take candy from strangers' rule but figured there was safety in numbers--plus we had no concept that he could actually be dangerous. But we all agreed on the coded signal to 'grab your ear and wiggle it' when any one of us felt like it was time to go. We saw the rumored fun-town room but mostly it was just a dingy basement with some stuff in it that kids liked...not some magical place after all. Later when the cops came around house to house and questioned us individually, we started to get the drift of who and what Charlie was. He'd been caught hurting younger kids a few streets away—kids from Army St.—a small section of military housing. Big mistake. You don't mess with kids of military folks because they will go commando on your ass (deservedly so)...Years later I had heard that he'd been beaten up badly (the perpetrators were never 'found') and had to wear a cuff a la Martha Stewart that basically imprisoned him in his own house. He had to register as a sex offender and had restraining orders galore. My friends and I were lucky that we were probably strangely 'too old' for Charlie's liking. The kids he'd been accused of hurting were 4 and 5 year olds apparently. Don't ask me how a four or five year old made it into some creepy guy's basement unattended unless it was with an older sugar-drugged, pinball-distracted sibling maybe?

But mostly it was a run-of-the-mill suburban neighborhood--I played with friends until the streetlights came on, and was tucked in with a story at night. So when I heard the sad and terrifying tales of the other hospital dwellers' kidhoods—I'd think back with a mixture of nostalgia and confusion to my own early beginnings which had been so benign in comparison. Why was I here? When had I derailed and detoured so off course that my path had led me here? And could I ever find my way back again to some feeling of innocence and hope? More questions I pondered between eating junk food, reading trashy novels and watching the same movies over and over again. It was like an adolescent's dream and nightmare rolled into one. All the free time and potato chips in the world yet no freedom to enjoy it. The common ground we all shared was being in the kind of pain that made us a danger to ourselves. The origins of that pain may've been drastically different but the pain was the thread that wove us all together in this weird tapestry of mental illness.

Though I may have had a slightly different upbringing than the other patients I was and am pretty run of the mill among my friends. One friend recently called me a hippie. I nearly bit his head off....which I tend to think is a decidedly un-hippielike thing to do. Sure I like dandelions, and yeah I grew up in the seventies, *man*. But hippie???!!! Do they even still exist in 2007? As I see it, we flower children have all grown up and we have a few different parameters and certainly updated terminology I should hope. Here was my shrill response (embellished a wee bit here for poetic license):"Hippie? Excuse me, but I will take airy-fairy, tree hugger or eccentric New Ager but I am NOT a hippie. Angels, crystals, tarot cards, Reiki yes, yes, and yes...but hello? I bathe regularly and Patchouli? Pa-YUCKY. And I do not smoke the ganga or have hemp clothing and I'm sorry, burning one's bra is just plain silliness. I paid a lot of good money for my bras (TMI?) and I am not about to burn my underwire, lacy number from Victoria's Secret or let the girls flap in the wind just to make some sort of feminist point. "I am woman, see me sag?"...I mean sure—if the whole ethanol fuel thing takes off and windmill energy-powered cities crop up everywhere then that's fabulous, but I think the only thing more annoying than a Vegan lifestyle would be well... frankly I can't think of anything more annoying. Because animals? Are delicious. And they make lovely shoes, belts and jackets at times, too. So there goes that argument."

Flower power used to mean 'revolution' and antidisestablishmentarianism (yes—it IS a big word for being a rebel or anarchist which are just polite terms for being a total pain in the ass)...Now it means a cute, floral-patterned top from Old Navy or picking up the occasional cheerful bunch of sunflowers to brighten the apartment. Does this make me shallow? Hey—I like Bob Dylan and John Lennon as much as the next gal. I am *all* for world peace. But I simply fail to see how me growing my armpit hair into smelly dreads will help achieve that crucial objective.Maybe neo-hippie is a more accurate label? Sorta seems like a combination yuppie/hippie. Or maybe even Yippie? *I'm a Yippie, You're a Yippie, He's a Yippie, She's a Yippie, Wouldn't ya like to be a Yippie, too?* Not sure about that one, though. It tends to conjure up small dogs and perky cheerleaders. But it'll do until something better comes along. Sure--I vote liberal and sometimes wear earth shoes and drink Starbucks and shop at Whole Foods...but you will *never* see me sporting a tie-dyed *anything*. And I will not be growing my own food in a container garden on my fire escape or be caught dead or alive chanting cumbaya around a campfire. I would sooner vote Republican. Cumbayall set.

Growing up, I can distinctly remember my health-conscious mother making yummy Rice Krispie treats with peanut butter, honey and raisins instead of the marshmallow and butter that other moms used to use. I can also distinctly recall the other kids at CCD (The Catholic after school version of religiously brainwashing kids...but with SNACKS) asking me if the raisins were bugs. In retrospect I realize that wasn't very Christian of them. But I think even Jesus snickered at that one. Needless to say I wasn't such a fan of the peanut butter/ honey snap, crackle and pop treats after that. In other words, in some things it pays to conform. When it comes to torching one's lingerie to prove one's equality with the half of the population who wear jock straps rather than brassieres... well...call me a rebel but I just don't see the point. So what would constitute a hippie today? Peace rallies are a wonderful idea in the abstract but I'd rather get Zen and meditate...envisioning a world in which people don't need to *rally* for peace...because their very essence embodies peace. I'd rather get together with like-minded people (or even differently minded people who can articulate their opinions well) to discuss how we can all achieve our creative goals and dreams than circulate emails about troops torturing small children. This isn't about being an ostrich or an idealist. It is a conscious choice to say 'pfffft' to the fearmongering media.The hybrid car is a wonderful idea. Recycling is extremely environmentally sound. It just makes sense. Waste not, want not and *hey—how about not turning Mother Earth's backyard into a giant landfill?* are valid principles to aspire to...But doing all those socially correct things and then engaging in the sociopathic kind of road rage where you are flipping off random strangers and cursing their as-yet unborn great-grandkids....hmmm, then perhaps the priorities are just a tiny smidgen skewed?

Someday, we shall overcome self-imposed stereotypes and limitations. We'll outgrow our labels and create bigger picture language. But in the meantime... please don't eat the daisies...or call me a hippie. Unless you want the peace sign I make to go from two fingers to one. Peace out.

One night at the women's center we were all minding our own business and watching American Idol when the fire alarm went off. Apparently, they were testing the system. Great idea—scare the shit out of a bunch of emotionally strung out women all in their PJs just before bedtime when most of them do relaxation exercises to wind down in the hope of warding off nightmares. After the system had been tested the irony factor kicked in. It worked alright—worked so well it wouldn't shut down and just kept screeching at earsplitting decibels. The snafu was due to some 'loose wiring' (more irony) and electricians would have to be called in to remedy the situation. So we were exiled, single file, to the hospital campus' main building which housed the cafeteria. We were a motley, ragtag group...women all ages, shapes, colors and sizes. We were promised that if we had to camp out the staff would get us a TV to pass the time and try and make us as comfortable as possible. It felt like the world's strangest sleepover. Just as some of us were starting to doze off (from boredom more than weariness) we were told the alarm had been fixed and we could return to the treatment center house. When the excitement had died down and we all were settled snug in our hospital-issue, crappy, springy beds I lay there in the dark, thinking and blinking. The tears came wave after wave threatening to engulf me because it was moments like this, nights like tonight that acutely reminded me of my caged status. While we were being shepherded to the cafeteria, it was hard to pretend that this was anything even remotely resembling a 'normal' scenario. When in the hospital I thought of myself as sick—like any other sick person in need of care. After that—having been discharged to a home-like environment where our groups were more like 'classes' it was easy to imagine it as a sort of college dorm of sorts. But being corralled into an atmosphere that didn't fit in with any of my 'glossing' self-deluding skills made it all seem too real somehow. I didn't really feel any common ground with the other women. I felt set apart from the 'community'. I'd tried to tell myself this was a good thing—not to form any lasting attachments here was probably healthy in the long run, etc. It gave me more time for contemplation and protected me from the inevitable sadness of leavetakings. I felt more alone that night than I ever have before. Then I heard a little tap on my door and a small voice squeaked out *"Are you ok?"* My sniffling and not quite pillow-stifled, hiccupping sobs had given me away.

My neighbor (also of the Yippie persuasion) and I had an hour-long, through-the-door, whispered conversation that felt like church confession without the priest. She had a sophisticated accent that was difficult to place. She told me that she was originally South African and had moved to France and then to Aruba where she currently lived with her lawyer husband and 'lovely' three children whom she dearly missed (yet also secretly enjoyed having a bit of a break from). She and her husband were splitting up and she was feeling horribly depressed and 'useless'. She'd been getting more and more listless and less and less able to take care of the children when her husband had signed her up (without consulting her) for this program on the suggestion of one of his golf buddies. She was so soft-spoken that I had to strain to hear even her whispers. We commiserated that night and went for a walk to the local coffee shop the next day. She told me that I seemed 'articulate and bright' (my forehead must send off some flashing invisible/subconscious signals to this effect since it was a compliment I received more times than I can remember during those dark days as though my being articulate and bright somehow meant I couldn't be so very sick after all, could I?). I would have preferred gorgeous and brilliant but articulate and bright was ok, too. I told her that I was sure her kids wouldn't ally with her slimy husband in a conspiracy against her. Sometimes she'd lapse into French and I'd lose her. Other times—I'd trail off into my own thoughts and she'd lose me. But mostly we were just able to be a war buddy kind of support for each other by talking and listening. Most of the other women noticed and commented on how her voice got stronger over time and her quiet shyness ceded to the occasional well-timed dry comment. And around her I felt a sense of calm like everything would be ok.

Sometimes, we'd catch each other's eyes and share an eye-roll, smirk or sardonically raised brow. When she left—a few months before I would be set free she gave me a beautiful postcard. It was a black and white shot of a boat stuck in ice. The image was haunting. She had written on it that she knew I felt like this boat sometimes but I was brave and strong and talented (and lots of other very sweet superlatives) and that the thaw would come.

And there was my common ground. It broke the ice (so to speak) for me to realize that attachment isn't always such a horrible thing even when it's with others who are suffering—call it codependent—I call it compassion... Only someone who has been to hell and back can understand the dark journey's twists and turns and this creates an unspoken code of understanding. I was woefully disappointed when she left but relieved for her sake that she'd be reunited with her children and was leaving prepared to stand up to her domineering husband. And she'd been a bright light that reached through a door and held my heart with her kindness. For that—I'd always be grateful for the stupid and annoying fire alarm that woke me up out of an emotional dead sleep and helped me turn a very important corner on that ever-shifting path to wellness.

Money, money, money, money.....money

The summer help. That's what my life had come to a few years ago-- it would seem that after having globe trotted, worked in advertising, health care, social services, and the corporate world now I was the summer help. Gone was my parents' and grandparents' era where buying a house was as easy as buying a car is today. I live in the world of renters....those of my friends who do have homes need both incomes to keep afloat and any sudden illness or life event could easily bring in the bank rubbing its hands together greedily for one or two missed mortgage payments. So in order to make ends more than meet so I could travel and have a social life that consisted of more than my couch and remote control and a stale bag of Cheetos, I took on extra jobs. Under the guise of house-sitting, pet-sitting and being an "extra set of hands" I was talked into doing a two-week stint in Wellfleet when a friend of a friend's nanny had canceled last minute... Fat lot of good the college degree was doing me as I washed my thousandth dish or threw in my millionth load of laundry. I tried to feel grateful and remind myself that no job was "beneath me" when it came to paying the bills. However the pulsating blisters on my feet (from the ill-fitting sandals I'd chosen to pack) were an obstacle to my Zen-like gratitude exercises. And to boot—I'd unceremoniously locked my keys in my car.

Triple A was called and now I was on my third cup of coffee as I awaited their arrival. *"Could be worse,"* I mused. *"I could be slathered with honey and eaten alive by red ants or strung up by my toenails and forced to belt out upside-down show tunes."* Instead, I stole this time before the kids woke up and the day began. I used to dream of living in a big house with many people to attend to all the little things. I loved fairy stories that had butlers and nannies and housekeepers in them, a team of foot soldiers of convenience always at the ready, anticipating needs and with a quiet dignity taking pride in their modest yet decent station in life. Roll-up-your-sleeves workers, but not without some solid sense of status. I wanted to have those people around me, not to become one of them. One of life's little karmic ironies.

Maybe all that early literature *had* gone to my head and filled it with delusions of grandeur. We grew up neither wealthy nor poverty stricken—we were the other, the middle class, the bourgeoisie. How I've always had contempt for that word. It seemed, like the middle child of the class family, bland and forgotten. We had shag, not plush carpet, and we had motels not five-star hotels. We ate fast food and drove economy cars. The rich drove fast cars and ate nouvelle cuisine. We'd comfort ourselves by reassuring each other that they weren't really happy. As though we believed that money had a taint or unpleasant odor to it. Yet we always scraped by and made payments on the private school tuition, the house, the braces, the vacations. The bills were our constant silent enemy companion. We were always hoping to rack up investments in a nebulous future where struggle wasn't part of the game anymore. My dad diligently sweated his face off mowing the lawn and my mother hunched over her flower bed as we played kickball until the streetlights came on. I was lucky to be fed, clean and well cared for so what was the source of this restlessness? Was it that prince/castle/plasma TV theory of happiness thing again? Those invisible promises for elusive happy endings punctuated by passionate kisses scented with minty fresh breath?

As kids, my family went to the drive-in in our station wagon and whined on long road trips in cars that had open window air-conditioning. We mini-golfed and go-carted and swooshed down water slides. We even did the Disney thing. We had rich relatives and poor ones. Ones who had summer beach homes by the sea and ones who couldn't pay their heating bill. There were a lot of mixed messages about money. I'm still sorting through them over 20 years later. We were greedy for the latest toy, game, experience. We ushered in the electronic era with Pong and Atari. Pinball became Pac-Man and Space Invaders. *The Brady Bunch* and *Little House on the Prairie* were our religion. The TV was our God. Santa was king. And Peter Pan was a perfectly acceptable role model urging us to "Never Grow Up."

Perhaps the idiot box was where my downfall into indentured servitude began. I watched for hours and hours. I absorbed endless advertisements and commercials subversively telling me I stank, I was fat and ugly and I needed this product or that to fix my broken, inadequate self. These were interspersed amongst mindless sitcoms and soap operas where the toothpaste smile actresses suffered agonizing heartaches over men with names like Renaldo and Blaine. Names that sounded more like appliances than people.

When I was fifteen, I worked in a submarine sandwich shop and baby-sat for pocket money. "Pin money" it would be called in a British novel. Again with the Anglophiliac identity crisis. I fancied myself Mary Poppins for awhile but rapidly realized that dirty diapers were not at all magical. I went to college and partied like John Belushi in *Animal House*. I traveled and studied abroad. I became a student of human nature. Which, apparently, and much to my dismay, doesn't translate into a job all that well, or at least not one that pays. I've worked in retail, the college coffee shop, I've temped in a million different office environments, stuffed zillions of envelopes and survived mass mailings, attended political galas where sharks in suits circle one another with their business cards... Public relations was particularly challenging and with all that spinning I ended up very dizzy and downhearted. I just need a break of some sort. Not a winning lottery ticket necessarily but maybe an intro to my future husband who just so happens to be a publishing mogul would be nice. Very nice. Betty Friedan and Gloria Steinem are shuddering with disgust somewhere. I am woman hear me whore...Traditional careers so far have eluded me and since I'm very well suited to the writing life and one does feel that tugging yearning for a partner to share it all with, I figure, you know, two birds, one stone and call it a day.

Anyway—where was I? Oh yes—Wellfleet. With one child who threw up on my shoes the very first hour of the first day I arrived and the other whose incessant, high-pitched whining could break even the strongest military general. Their mother was playing tennis and dad stayed behind in the city to "get some work done"...which sounded suspiciously like a mystery mistress but how the hell would I know and it's not nice to make assumptions, right? Even if they were confirmed later by a reliable source. Tennis mom turned out to be a bitch from hell and I wound up telling her where she could stick her racket...needless to say the job ended early and my stint as the summer help was over before I could say "Jeeves." Even now—I spend lots of time and energy trying to pin money down. To see it merely as green paper and bits of metal alloy. A means to an end. A form of energetic exchange. And to little by little eradicate the clenching fear that I'll never have "enough" to feel "safe." Which is ridiculous, really. Because I am safe. And I do have pocket money. I may have to stretch it so thin that you could blow smoke through it sometimes, but I am not begging on the streets just yet. But another stressor that added to my overall garage experience was feeling constantly squeezed by bill collectors and never getting ahead, let alone caught up. I know I could manage my resources a lot better. I mean a *lot* better. Just ask my poor dad who has tried to give me the "here's how you figure out your monthly expenses" speech more times than I can count. Just not good at math all around I guess. I can never seem to wade through the credit card offers that appear beckoning me like travel agents to visit the mountains of debt. I usually just throw them away without opening them and getting lost in their teeny tiny fine print—which probably says you have to have sex with a three-legged goat to break the contract or something equally disgusting like paying tons of exorbitant hidden fees that could keep one of those horrifyingly sad kids with flies crawling on their faces in bling-bling that JAY-Z would envy.

Hopefully someday I'll be out from under money's siren song spell and realize that it isn't about having a team of people to "do" for you (though for the record I would not turn that down if offered), it's about cultivating other forms of currency that are intangible. Time, love, peace, friendship. laughter...But let's face it—a Ferrari wouldn't hurt, either.

Fringe Benefits

There are some advantages to being considered crazy. Apart from the lovely "Club Med" spa vacations where attendants pamper you with pills and shock treatments, there is also that "whatever" factor. As in you can do or say "whatever" and people won't be too fazed. Heading into my second month in the hospital I was put on a drug to help me manage my carb cravings brought on by one of my other medications. This tiny white pill had an interesting effect. It gave me a break from reality. A little "psychotic break" to be specific. Apparently, I still walked and looked like Courtney—but the words coming out of Courtney's mouth were not what we would call typical. Contrary to popular belief—one does not have to be violent to be psychotic—merely very "altered" in their speech or behavior. I was altered alright. I vaguely remember a consult with a female and male doctor where I reached out to join their hands claiming that they were soulmates and wishing them well. Since both of them had respective spouses at home they were not tickled by my sudden matchmaking skills. I have been told by friends that I was jabbering a lot more New Age stuff than usual and had shared some disturbing thoughts like wondering what might happen internally to my organs if I swallowed my ring. I think that one came from the girl at the school I worked at who had threatened to swallow a shard of glass.

The consensus was that I should get off this drug immediately and wrestle my carb cravings another way. At the time I chose smoking more cigarettes—not the smartest move but it did work temporarily until the hacking cough and yellow teeth became the natural deterrent to that little solution. Having recently stopped the ECT and now withdrawing from this not-so-happy drug, I was a complete, quivering mess. At night, I didn't sleep—even with sleep meds, during the day, however, I slept a lot—wandering into the kitchen for the occasional meal or the common room for the occasional group...but I mainly existed in a foggy in-between reality and fantasy place where nothing I said or did made any sense.

Slowly but surely I came out of the fog into another place—depression. My chemistry was going so haywire and it brought me really low. I had crying jags on and off for days. It was like the worst case of PMS hormonal shifts ever. Anything could set me off and there was plenty of sadness-inducing stimuli all around me. When I spent an hour with the woman with the Disney character fetish whose fiancé had died leaving her wanting to follow him to that great theme park in the sky—I was a snotty, hiccupping mess from all of the tears deluging from my face. She ended up reassuring me that she was safe and wouldn't act on her death wish that night so it'd be ok and begged me to stop crying since then she'd start up again, too. And then there was the 19-year-old gay boy whose family couldn't accept his orientation and the ex-stripper/drug addict who was involved with a man almost three times her age—I don't know if that one made me sad or just freaked me out (probably a little bit of both). Sitting with them was surreal and I kept thinking that if I hadn't tried to kill myself I'd never have met these interesting folks or heard their sad tales. It wasn't exactly a silver lining but it was something.

Apart from colorful characters with colorful stories there were also plenty of "ordinary" people (not the movie—that's a whole other depressing rant). There was a teacher, a lawyer, a scientist and a wealthy businesswoman. Our lives had all intersected and overlapped in this weird place for these weird moments and soon it became oddly (and even comfortingly at times) "normal." I'd like to say that after an extended stay in a mental hospital that nothing will ever faze me again—but I know it's not true. It was, however, an experience made of memorable conversations you're not likely to have in your everyday life.

"So my kid found the gun I was gonna use in my desk drawer and my wife said it was either sign myself in or get myself a good lawyer. I didn't have the money for an ambulance chaser so here I am."

"My social worker says I can only stay here for a few days this time because my insurance is running out but at least by then my ex might be down off his bender."

"I work as a dancer...the pole is kinda like a friend...people don't understand how lost in the music I get. I don't feel exploited when I dance...I feel graceful and beautiful...and I'm in control...not the other way around. When I feel depressed I go home to my big house with my big hot tub and I just close my eyes and think of my next routine, about what moves I want to change or add."

But they were not all depressing conversations or depressing stories. Some people simply viewed their hospital time as a rest cure much like in old-fashioned Victorian stories where people went to the seaside for the restorative properties of fresh air and sunshine. But instead of fresh air and sunshine, we had fluorescent lighting and dusty vents.

I came to realize that even suicidal people craved little, everyday comforts. While we may have given up on life or any foreseeable future—we'd sure like a soft bed and better water pressure in the shower. I, for one, would have loved a toothbrush that didn't leave my gums bleeding every time I used it. And sure, there were always things that visitors could smuggle in from time to time but it just wasn't the same. It is true--you cannot buy freedom. I may not have been a political prisoner living under a harsh dictatorship, but I did feel "institutionalized" in every sense of the word. How a place could have such schedules and routines yet still hours and hours of stretching nothingness seemed virtually impossible. You'd lose all track of time and visits were both craved and dreaded. It was a lovely distraction—but a humiliating one. I am blessed with many wonderful friends and a family who were/are incredibly supportive (despite my sister's reticence and cool withdrawal at the time—I always knew she secretly loved me and ached for me even if she was too proud or angry then to admit it).

Early on, I did half-jokingly tell one friend who "signed me out"—like a library book or whatever—for a walk, that we could just quickly and quietly walk to her car, get in and drive away. I quipped that I'd always wanted to be an "escaped mental patient." She wasn't buying it. I think I may have frightened her a bit to be totally honest.

I had my endless stream of greeting cards and little bath gels and my favorite foods—so really who was I to complain? There was one girl on the locked ward who did laundry all day long. For hours and hours on end. I think it soothed her or something. And she never had one visitor that I could recall. So she probably needed the distraction, too. Washing the same clothes over and over again? What's sadder than that?—except maybe the fact that she got reprimanded for tying up the machines. It broke my heart. But listening to the nightly collective whining session that happened during the nightly "community meeting" made me realize that we had all lost sight of the big picture somewhat. Well that's sort of an obvious statement now isn't it? The complaints were never-ending. I remember again that there always seemed to be a lack of enough milk. Apparently crazy people must have an increased need for calcium or something—either that or it was the high volume of coffee and cereal consumption. Decaf, of course. We were not allowed caffeine which drove me nuts, too (in a manner of speaking). On my occasional outings I'd latte up and screw it if my sleep was disrupted a little (I never seemed to sleep anyway so I might as well get a caffeine buzz out of it.) The java was a nice escape from the sedated feeling the meds often induced. Some of the sleep meds actually left a sort of hangover the next day which to me seemed rather counterproductive. Bad cycle—tired all day, half-awake all night—now that'll mess with your biorhythms for sure, my friend. Add some other chemicals to the mix and voila—permanent jet lag!

So, the creature comforts mattered. We now knew how much we had taken for granted in our former lives including the whole "shaving unsupervised" thing or being able to carry a lighter. For the smokers, the staff member who "walked" us in a loop around the campus at night or even during daylight hours regularly, would be the official lighter holder. He/she would then lend out the lighter one at a time always being sure to get it back by the end of the walk while we were trudging back to our incarceration. It was a fun little ritual. I suppose it wasn't the worst idea since with a lighter and unreliable brain chemistry we would officially be considered "armed and dangerous" more from the faulty grey matter wiring than the butane itself. But hey—put the two together and you have a potential crisis on your hands. I jest, but there was nothing funny about the burn or razor scars on some of the arms of those who indulged in these little moments of excruciating terror as either self-punishment or a reminder that they were alive and not invisible...made of flesh and not just fear. I asked one fellow resident after seeing her scars why she'd done it and she said that she was numb when she did it and didn't even remember it. I told her I still didn't really understand since I vividly remembered every single second of getting my tattoo and that was sort of self-inflicted, too, in a way. She just gave me a Mona Lisa smile and shrugged. No comparison I guess.

If you'd asked me during that time what material thing I missed the most, I would've been hard pressed to answer. Yes—a comfortable bed would be easier to sleep in and that would've been welcome considering my stupid and persistent insomnia issue. Vegetables that weren't canned or hadn't been cooked until the colors leached out of them and they only resembled distant cousins of their former fresh selves was something I missed too, I suppose. But mostly I had longings of a different kind. I sorely and dearly missed my sanity. I didn't really know what that meant, but it left me bereft and lonely to think about. I missed the simplicity of waking up having hope and the belief that things could and would get better.

I missed not living in this perpetual grey zone. At that time—I truly didn't live for myself. I lived so I wouldn't cause any more pain to the people who loved me and who were battling and struggling with me and for me. I missed wanting to live for living's sake. The rest of the stuff was just...stuff. So while I existed tentatively on the outer fringe of life, I learned that wellness is not only a state of mind or just about being able to "function." It's reflected back to you in the eyes of those you love. And that's better than a soft pillow or toothbrush any day.

Staff of Life

If the treatment program I was in sometimes seemed like a sort of zombie sleep-away camp, then the staff were the counselors, both literally and figuratively. At times staff and clients alike would all convene for a weekly group meeting to discuss any issues in the community that needed addressing. Unlike the hospital gatherings these were much longer and more articulate whine-fests. It was usually an opportunity for someone to drone on and on about the rights and privileges of the residents vs. the commuters. Since there was the overnight stay price differential it became a mini-war over burning issues like-- Was it fair for the daytime clients to use the peanut butter when technically they hadn't paid for it? Do I hear the strains of "*We are the world*" humming in the background? Um not exactly. The UN it was not. Or maybe it was. Often the issues started off as petty but became a larger philosophical debate about respect, boundaries and you guessed it—milk for the coffee. I can say with full confidence that somehow, in some behind-the-scenes way, the dairy industry is linked to the budget cuts in the mental health care system. Without a doubt. The one or two vegans and vegetarians were catered to and this also caused a bit of a ruckus. Wasn't a disproportionate amount of the budget going to their specialized dietary needs and shouldn't they pay more for their extra "special" meals that were time-consuming and wasteful, as they often ended up half eaten? These were the kinds of questions debated by our tribal council. At length. At *great* length. Week after week. Again and again. Getting the picture? Five months of this is more than enough to make anyone crazy and a crazy person even crazier.

So the lines were drawn—residents vs. daytimers and, of course, the ever-waging battle of staff vs. clients. It was interesting at first to note the interpersonal, group dynamics. But that quickly wore off. And by quickly I mean after the first two weeks. Some of the other clients who'd been discharged from lock-up around the same time I had would catch my eye from time to time as if to say—we thought this would be so much better? Sure we technically had more freedom to come and go—signing ourselves out on the whiteboard and checking in with the appointed staff member on duty. But now we endured an imprisonment of a different kind. We were now with folks who were supposedly "higher functioning" and that meant bigger egos, more interaction (less individual time to think) and the day was structured more rigorously here. No daytime naps unless you were sick or having a rough time while changing meds. But at least here it made sense that we were encouraged to stay awake all day so that by the time lights out rolled around we'd actually be tired.

The head of the program was a German woman, very attractive in an Eva Braun, hair always pulled back, sort of severe way, who was soft-spoken but known to be tough and unyielding. Most of the women wanted her steely aloofness, they tried to get her attention...

"Julia, see what I made today in Art Therapy? The colors represent the chaos I was feeling...remember the stuff that we talked about in our last session? I really feel like I had a breakthrough." They hovered around her hoping some of her tightness would wind them together and knit their unraveling souls and minds.

Julia always just gave her enigmatic tight smirk and nodded slightly...as though no matter what you were saying she couldn't care less....like a distracted mother of twelve children....not wanting to over-praise one above the others, she left them all wanting for more....attention, approval...to be noticed and acknowledged. So it was back to group therapy and try to get their needs met in the larger setting they went.

That much group time and talking, specifically often about emotionally draining topics, sometimes led to personality clashes and outbursts. Many a client left a group in a huff over something triggering that had been said, leaving us all in a cloud of dust. Finally these adolescent dramatics were addressed in one of the larger group meetings and acknowledged as disrespectful to the others, and it was decided that it was important to try and stay through the group at all costs. Once the doors were closed they were to remain so just as though we were always at the Opera. And it wasn't that different than an opera, truth be told. Aside from the angry storm-outs, bathroom breaks were to be limited to the 5 minute between group time breaks. However, one day I had missed getting in (there was often a long line—40 women 2 bathrooms, 5 minutes—you do the math) and had drunk a fair amount of coffee. I was squirming like a toddler and finally asked the group leader permission to go to the bathroom. She gently asked me to attempt to hold it. I tried but ended up apologizing and leaving two minutes later. I was both humiliated and angry—not at the group leader who was a good five years younger than me, but at the absurdity of the situation. When I was locked up and my freedom supposedly more limited—if I had to pee I could—at any given time. Plus the groups there were a lot shorter and there were more bathrooms available so this never became an issue really. I was pissed (pun intended) as I washed my hands and prepared to enter the classroom but went up to my room to calm down instead. I was 32 years old. I determined that I would never, ever ask someone to relieve my bladder as long as I lived. I vowed this to myself. I would simply get up and excuse myself saying that I'd be right back. In any given situation. After all, I had never been a door slammer (well at least not in this program—family skirmishes aside—they don't count here) and therefore here I was being punished for the histrionics of others. To say I regressed slightly and for a few hours and indulged my inner pouty, two-year-old, fuming about life's general unfairness might be a fair assessment. To say I overreacted—no I don't think skipping the next three classes, hiding out in my room and reading was an inappropriate response to this annoying *"Mother May I?"* happenstance. To say I "vented"—ok there might have been some yelling, about this situation during my nightly staff check-in would about sum it up. Mostly, my therapist and I, who rehashed it all later, agreed that it was a sign of returning health that I got angry about my independence being so compromised and that it merely signaled that I was indeed on the road to recovery. After I calmed down I did think that going easier on the coffee might not be a bad idea.

But there was to be another time that I lost my freedom privileges in such a painful and palpable way that I did actually throw a fit. Quite literally. I was again going through some med tweaking and "titrating" and was a bit "altered" again. I was revved like a NASCAR engine and sleeping, which had been on and off and at least I had been sure to get 4 hours minimum per night, was suddenly out of the question. I was officially hypo-manic. Slightly relieved that I wasn't psychotic (that's a fun feeling—"well at least I'm not psychotic" is not ever something you want to think, really), I confessed in a family therapy session (yes, these were mandatory since my parents had "found" me during the attempt they were traumatized, too, and it was deemed necessary and at times helpful—but mostly god-awful and in my mind a fitting "punishment" for my sin—that old Catholic voice persisted) that I was starting to have racing thoughts again. The social worker asked me if I was "*safe*" and I had to admit that I didn't know. Safe was code for—at what level are your self-harm thoughts—are they manageable or starting to get out of control? So the psychologist did the worst thing ever. And probably the best now that I have the gift of hindsight. He asked me for my keys. I was appalled, indignant and terrified. Taking my link to the outside world was like sending me back into lockup. It was having someone watch me shave, hold a lighter for me because I wasn't allowed my own, an annoying twenty-something waking me up when I wanted to sleep forever, lightning zaps to the brain, and asking in kindergarten-like fashion if I could pee—ALL ROLLED INTO ONE!!!!!! I finally had gotten to a level of trust where I could drive myself to CVS, the grocery store and the coffee shop and now we were going backwards???!!! I politely declined (OK I think by politely declined I really mean I told him no fucking way, thanks very much—so at least I added the thanks part) and asked what plan B was. He told me he'd get me in to see the doctor ASAP for a med consult and she'd work with me but asked me again for my keys as a safety promise. My parents chimed in on the plea and now it was three to one. I was the cheese and baby, I sure as hell was standing alone on this one. After some more attempted (but failed) verbal manipulation on my part—my outings to the library to check my email had become a necessary daily ritual, it wasn't my fault that this new med wasn't working it was the doc's fault—go ask her for her damned keys instead if you're suddenly so eager to start a key collection but buddy you ain't getting mine. After my rant there was a black silence in the room that hung there for about 2 full minutes—which can be a lifetime when three people are looking at you with fear, disappointment and expectation. Finally I gave in, threw the keys angrily at his feet and said "*Take them, then,*" choking back the sobs.

My parents' combined sigh of relief was audible and reminded me what we were all going through was a nightmare far beyond any of our comprehension. It was a battle won by a staff member. A decision that he'd made had most likely saved my life. Didn't stop me from haunting and taunting him relentlessly for the next week (even enlisting help from the other clients who were all too willing to jump on the "free Courtney's keys" bandwagon) until I got them back. But later after I got off that horrible med I was grateful and told him so. Another incident about three weeks later makes me laugh because of its contrast. I was doubting myself and my level of "safety" and tough love nurse sensed it and I said, *"I don't know if I can drive—I'm really shaken up"*. She told me to calm down a bit and then just go do my errands--it would be a good distraction, reassuring me that surely there were plenty of idiots out there on the road who were far worse drivers than me and then she actually, even playfully, winked at me. Here was softie guy who'd laid down the law uncharacteristically and toughie chick who'd told me everything would be ok. And it reminded me so much of my parents and how sometimes they'd pull this role reversal on you out of the clear freakin' blue and you wouldn't know what to think. Be careful. Have fun. Be independent—but still need us. Love others but love us more. I knew it was projection or transference or some other Freudian thing but it didn't matter. I had my keys back and I was going driving. The open road had never felt so good.

Generation Gaps

Being almost exactly the median age of the treatment house inhabitants, sometimes it was funny to watch the dynamics unfold between both the younger and older staff members and the younger and older clients—and all the crossover in between. I was the big/little sister or aunt figure in a house full of mothers and daughters. Even though we could all kick into maternal nurturing role when needed, there were a few wise elders who seemed like unofficial chiefs and not much seemed to faze them. One woman was particularly often cast in this role again and again. She'd lost her adult son to leukemia and on the days she wasn't banging her head against the wall crying about it (perfectly natural reaction to such a horror and we all gave her leeway and tissues during these episodes—someone even had the foresight to put a pillow against the wall and hold her hands to keep her from literally tearing her hair out in clumps). Other than these episodes, she embodied a peacefulness that attracted us all to her like a magnet. She didn't lose her cool more than a handful of times over the course of several months...(she was the only person who'd been there longer than me and stayed almost a year in total. When she did have a freakout, it was a big, loud, weepy wailing mess—but then it would be over and the storm would pass and she'd feel better for a few weeks. She would often try and bake away her pain. She baked and baked until the house always smelled of brownies or cinnamon buns or banana bread or some other confection. When the house smelled like that for a week straight, we knew E. was really suffering. An ex-hippie (the real deal) who knew all about different cultures and had marched in the 60s, she was fond of all different kinds of music. When E. had stopped baking and took to her bed for three days, her closest friend decided that if the staff members weren't helping her (not for lack of trying but they just weren't getting through) then we'd all have to rally and get her smiling again—or at least out of bed.

So we all padded upstairs in our pajamas, gathered in her room and sat cross-legged on the floor. Tightly packed in we swayed gently against each other, shoulder to shoulder...We started singing "*We shall overcome*" (hey—it wasn't Cumbaya so I was ok) and the tears streaming down her face switched from sorrow to joy and gratitude after the first refrain. She sat up and joined in--the loudest of all of us and we matched her conviction and volume and the echoes hummed through our ears and up our spines and tingled our toes. We were there for over a half hour in tune with each other, the moment, aligning with all of the passion that the song had held for all those who felt trampled on who had ever sung it...It was a very moving experience until one of us piped up—"-*Ladies—have we overcome, yet? My back is killing me from sitting on this floor.*" Ok I confess—it was me but from the group laugh I got and nods of agreement, I think we all felt it was time to get E. downstairs. After all—there was baking to be done. No—really—we told her we'd missed her and asked her to get up and rejoin the world—our world which had an E.-sized hole in it, and she wiped her tears and thanked us, telling us that nobody had ever done anything so kind and sweet and selfless like that before for her, and she almost started crying all over again. Her friend rerouted that potential disaster by telling E. that she loved her dearly, but after having been bedridden for days she stank and sorely needed a shower and that it would perk her up besides. E. chuckled amiably and agreed, shooing us all out and gathering her shower gear and some fresh clothes. I can honestly say that we younglings, and I count myself in that group because apart from the few teens and early twentysomethings it was mostly women in their late 40s-early 60s in that room, learned or remembered quite a beautiful lesson that morning. That we *would* overcome. That we would continue to fight the good fight, wielding pills and talk therapy and self help books (and Oprah of course) as our chosen battle weapons. Tragedy and sympathy go hand in hand but compassion is an altogether different thing. It's a living thing—it breathes, it sings and it sits cross-legged when it has a bad back. For the next few weeks it wasn't uncommon to hear someone humming that inspirational tune under their breath or singing it softly in the kitchen when doing dishes. It's a catchy tune and it caught on like wildfire—it became our theme song resurrecting its original meaning and giving it a new twist. It's a song of freedom but we were not free, at least not in the true sense yet. It's a song of hope and lots of times we were not hopeful, either. But it was a love letter to E. and to ourselves and every time she heard it she smiled. She said it made her feel young and strong again. It reminded her of a time in her life where everything was about exploration and experimentation. About rebellion. And about testing yourself and others—seeing where you ended and they began. Finding and constantly recreating your identity. And leaving room for new ideas by embracing change and growth in all its forms.

On the other end of the age spectrum was someone who still embodied these ideals. Susie bounced around with her glossy, long red hair and Lindsay Lohan-like looks, sporting her baby-Ts imprinted with messages like *"I'm a bad girl—you better spank me"*... She seemed like any other 17-year old until we found out that her boyfriend had OD'd and died and that she'd tried to kill herself shortly thereafter in Romeo and Juliet fashion. She was so bubbly and effervescent that the rest of us enjoyed her antics—but were also slightly suspicious that it was an act. She claimed it was just her personality to be upbeat and "positive" but she was depressed sometimes, too, really. Her best friend was also in the hospital but in another program for eating disorders housed across campus. They text messaged each other all day long, ate lunch together and hung out together whenever possible. The other women would often make comments about how could her mother let her leave the house in such tight clothes--but I just defended her saying that it was the style and we all knew that if we had bodies like that then we'd want to show them off too. That one quieted the room pretty quickly. I liked Susie. She was fun and sweet and meant no harm, really. Her only real crime was that she was young and seemingly happy despite her protestations. I think a lot of the envy stemmed from the fact that—yes—she'd suffered through a tragedy and subsequently gotten very ill herself—but she was young enough and pretty enough—she'd bounce back. But what about us? they accused with their gossiping, jealous eyes. She was treated mostly like a sorority girl or Dallas cheerleader at an NPR convention. I hated it but could only be nice to her as recompense and found that it wasn't hard. Some of her bubbliness was nervousness and I found she was much more low-key and easy to talk to one on one. She asked me all kinds of questions about my travels and my New Age beliefs—did I know that Kabbalah stuff, too? I told her that I hadn't gotten around to that really or I had but didn't have a great experience. I told her about the humiliating time I asked a local rabbi if I could join a Kabbalah class who immediately informed me I had mispronounced it but agreed to let me sit in for one session to try it out. I really enjoyed the class and learned quite a bit, but it was as if this woman could smell "shiksa" on me and asked me to stay after the others had left. She asked me how I'd liked the class and before I could ask her a question about something, she turned the tables and grilled me about my motives. If I hadn't grown up Jewish, why was I interested in this text—was it only because it was trendy? Because of Madonna? I assured her that I'd always been curious about all religions and I said that if it made her uncomfortable then maybe I shouldn't return. She said I should go and examine my motives more closely and perhaps join a different group somewhere else. I only remember thinking it ironic that a female rabbi was so conservative.

Susie was floored by that story—*"Omigod like she kicked you out of Kabbalah class after one time? Just 'cause you aren't Jewish? What a total bitch?!"* I answered that I was sure that if someone who was non-Catholic showed up in a class about the Virgin Mary and they thought it was just because of the da Vinci code--the priest or nun would probably have the same knee-jerk reaction. People are protective and defensive about their faith these days for lots of different reasons—scandals and terrorism being only a few. She agreed and understood that while I'd initially been somewhat mystified by the rabbi's reaction, I later realized it wasn't about her or about me or an ancient sacred text, even--it was about respect. I gently then led into a discussion about what I'd learned: that it really means to respect your elders and how certain people who grow up at certain times think that certain things are offensive—simply because that's the way they were raised and they deserved sympathy—not anger—for not being able or willing to stretch their minds--it was just habit and fear of losing their cherished traditions. She was thinking about it when I went in for the kill. Like, for example I loved the sassy Gap and Old Navy t-shirts she wore and thought they were adorable and looked great on her—but maybe, just maybe, some of the sayings were not...and look...I told her...I hated this word as much as if not more than she did... "appropriate" in a setting where lots of women had been sexually abused or even raped. She gasped in horror and smacked her forehead wincing. She claimed that she had never even thought about it and she thanked me for bringing it to her attention. From that day forward she would wear... *"like...normal clothes or whatever"* and the last thing she wanted to do was upset people. I reassured her that no—I did not think she was a bad person for wearing these t-shirts but yes I agreed with her wise decision and from there I changed the subject.

After that when she started wearing the "like normal clothes or whatever"... some of the tensions towards her eased and I felt glad that I'd played some small part in the fact that now the women could stop focusing on her flippant beauty and on her sweet charm instead. It was always better when we bonded rather than skirmished. But the skirmishes were normal, they were necessary to define and express who we were and what we were all about. Our differences were sometimes insurmountable. But most of the time the age thing wasn't such a big issue—after all, we were all women and had more in common than we realized until someone pointed it out. And someone would always play peacemaker whether a staff member or another coolheaded client when the gap seemed too wide. Yes there were slamming doors and silent dinners—just like in any family. We may have been an improvised, substitute family. We may even have often been dysfunctional, but we did our best to always try and meet somewhere in the middle.

Kicking English Muffins

If Susie's style of dress had seemed provocative then nobody was even remotely prepared for Tina. Next to Tina we all looked like nuns or women from another century in our clothing choices. A Eurasian beauty, she was an ex-stripper (complete with fake nails, colored contacts and plastically enhanced DD boobs) married to a man three times her age. Insert *'ewwww'* here...She was clearly more LA than Boston, more Hollywood than New England and more nightclub than workaday like the rest of us. In fact, she and her husband now co-owned the club where they'd met. At the time she'd been 13 and he was a manager with aspirations to buy. Oh yes—that was age thirteen I wrote—that's not a typo. It was a Dickensian tale with a Roman Polanski twist. Apparently, according to Tina—they'd never dated until she was 18...nobody breathed a sigh of relief at that information. One night as I raided the kitchen for some sugary comfort, Tina was in there, too and we got chatting. Well—she got chatting and I 'umm..hmmmed' between bites of Ben and Jerry's. She told me that she was used to the mingled horror and shocked responses she got whenever she talked about her colorful past—or her colorful present for that matter. I got quite an education from her impromptu lecture on the mechanics of pole dancing and how whenever she danced she felt 'free'. She missed the pole more than she missed her husband—I left that one alone biting my tongue so hard I thought it might bleed.

Here was another tightly clothed, shapely beauty and many of the women also complained about her style of dress to the staff but she refused to tone it down saying that this was America fer crissakes wasn't it? And we were all here to heal so maybe people should be focusing on that rather than superficial (or in this case artificial) things like her tits. She made a good point. The complaints shifted from her clothing to her incessant chatter. Everyone was a potential audience to her constant need to be in the spotlight. She'd transitioned from the dance floor where she got endless attention and flattery from drooling men offering to buy her cars, jewelry and clothes to a group of unimpressed women who wished she'd just shut up already. She became the target of vicious gossip (surprise, surprise) and over time it escalated to epic proportions. Most of it centered around her imagined promiscuity to drug use to good old fashioned gold-diggery. She had long, loud, repetitive cellphone conversations with her husband which became a fresh source for complaints. People didn't think she was a 'bad person' as they'd consistently assert...just a bad seed it seemed was the underlying critical tone that came through. She was further and further scapegoated as the sole reason for the lack of harmony in the house and the subsequent frissons of tension that grew with each new pair of butt-hugging jeans, skimpy top and bout of verbal diarrhea.

The phenomenon of the blessing/curse syndrome of having 'that kind of face' makes me privy to the trials and tribulations of the underdog in all walks of life. Tina sensed this and went in for the kill. Sensing a potential ally in me, or at least not an out and out hostile enemy, she shamelessly wooed me as a friend inviting me to her house, which apparently had a 'kickass hot tub'. I politely declined but told her I'd go to the grocery store one day when she cornered me and I couldn't think up a viable excuse. As we walked down the aisles I made a show of stopping from time to time pretending to read labels so I could give my neck a break from nodding like a bobblehead doll while she nattered on and on. As we cruised into the bread aisle she was in the midst of some story I'd already heard three times when I noticed a packet of English muffins on the floor further down the aisle. As we neared, I was about to bend over to retrieve it but she, never ceasing her monologue, kicked it violently out of the way, stepped around it and kept forging ahead. I stopped in my tracks and asked her why she'd done that? She laughed and said that she didn't realize that she'd done it but it had been in her way. So I bent over, picking it up and returning it to the shelf thinking about what she had said. I didn't judge her for what she'd done. I didn't really care. What I noticed most was that both of us were acting on instinct…she on hers and me on mine. What was the good girl instinct getting me in life? I didn't have bling, or own a nightclub or have a hot tub in my house. I wasn't married, I didn't have men drooling over me and I was actually—to be honest—lonely as hell. Just as she must have been, even with all of her toys and accoutrements because I don't care who you are—*nobody but nobody* talks that much and is that graspingly needy unless they are deeply unhappy with themselves and their life. So if the English muffins represented an obstacle in the path—my way was to politely remove it while hers was to kick it aside pretending it didn't exist and keep steaming ahead. I actually managed to insert this metaphor miraculously into the conversation when she stopped to take a breath and read a yogurt container. I said that wasn't it interesting--our different styles could be shown so blatantly with an English muffin pack…and I was careful to note that I in no way thought either way was better or more effective. She cocked her head to the side and considered it, sort of amused and confused all at the same time. She was eerily quiet on the ride back to the women's center. I asked her what was wrong and she said she was just thinking about the English muffin thing and how I was right—she did tend to just kick things aside and walk around them rather than take the time to notice or resolve them and she thought this might be a big insight into her character, her marital problems etc. and she thanked me for pointing it out.

OK—here I was two for two in the insight department and starting to feel like I should either 'graduate' to freedom soon, get my own talk show or be made a staff member. Yes—my ego swelled a little out of control I must admit. But there were always plenty of humbling moments at the treatment house to bring you back down to earth and later that night I'm sure someone yelled at me for taking too long to get ready for bed and tying up the bathroom or something equivalent, thus reminding me who and where I was. I was not the next incarnation of Freud. I was a mental patient who had gone grocery shopping with another mental patient who had kicked some English muffins. I was not everybody's surrogate wise, older sister ready to dispense life advice. I was sick, too. And I didn't even have a pole to miss. From that night on I deftly avoided Tina. Her exhausting presence left me grouchy and deflated. And I'm not just talking about my bosom, either. So I gave myself permission to stop tendering to the underdog and to start ministering to my own wounds that were left politely on a shelf next to some dusty English muffins. I stayed in my room reading that evening and of course had another semi-sleepless night. I was wound up from the Tina encounter and remembered Melinda Ross from the fifth grade. A girl that no one ever befriended, I'd brought her home one day and proceeded to try and cheer her up. Pity is never a solid foundation on which to base a budding friendship, however, and so halfway through the play date I wanted to strangle her for her contradictory, know-it-all arrogance and suddenly realized that the reason she was unpopular was not her plain looks and geeky mannerisms—it was her obnoxiousness and superhuman ability to annoy. What I had mistaken for quiet shyness was a hawk like observer making mental notes on people's flaws and dislikes only to in Machiavellian manner deconstruct them later in her self-imposed solitude. She just didn't like people. I now know this was probably some kind of self-protective, angry pre-adolescent device, but at the time I just thought her mean-spirited and petty. Needless to say—I felt I'd failed my mission to get to know her better and maybe share our love of books since I'd noticed her nose was always buried in one, too. We had nothing in common though, as even our reading tastes were dramatically different. After Melinda—I'd vowed never again to try and instigate a friendship as if approaching a school project. People weren't projects and the mingled shame I felt at myself and my own actions (inviting her over under false pretenses while secretly feeling 'saintly' for doing so) was only rivaled by the irritation I felt now every time I saw her face and had flashbacks of the time she'd come to my house and sat like a lump, bitterly complaining about everything, intermingled with long, awkward, brooding silences. I was reminded of this lesson with Tina...Just because someone is 'interesting' or 'colorful' doesn't make him or her the best candidate for friendship. And in the end it turned out that her self-involved blathering made her rather boring really. But by the same token, just because someone's having a hard time didn't mean I wouldn't befriend them, either. I made some lasting ties there during my 6-month stretch. But English muffin chick just wasn't destined to be one of them I'm afraid. So I decided to put her back on the shelf and keep on walking.

Getting the drift

One friend I had on the outside had a particularly rough time coming to visit and was one of the aforementioned 'angry' people at what I'd tried to do. She had a more than valid excuse. At age 9 she'd found her mother in the bathtub, wrists streaming crimson and an empty booze bottle on the ground. She dragged her semi-conscious mother out, wrapped her arms in towels and managed to call 911—all the while knowing that she was no longer a child—she was suddenly an adult and her mother was now the child who needed care. After an early trauma like that I didn't expect her to understand. Even though she'd long ago forgiven her mother and realized that she had been 'extremely ill'—which to her before this incident had meant having a really bad puking flu or cancer or something, she was still scarred from this memory and carried it with her always. This same friend had then gotten pregnant at 16, married at 18 (not to the father of her child) and proceeded to spend the next decade and a half repeating her own mother's mistakes. She was a genius—literally. Never went to college but inhaled books like oxygen. She and I had commiserated for years over the severe good man shortage even though she attracted them like flies to honey. I was a little subtler in my approach. She tried to teach me the 'sex stare'...the sex stare consisted of holding a man's glance for a few beats longer than normal. I never did quite get that one down. The men I used it on were baffled and asked if I was ok?...They wondered if they had something in their teeth or a booger hanging out of their nose. Not exactly the erotic effect I'd been going for. But she and I drank wine and smoked cigarettes while she tried to unravel the enigma of the male mystery (my true smoker friends hate my ability to smoke socially or even regularly for a few months—sometimes making a few packs last almost that long and then go cold turkey). She told me I was overthinking the whole dating thing and that if it didn't have to do with breasts, cars, beer or their penises men weren't generally interested much. I snottily protested that this was surely a limited stereotype and maybe it was true of the men she dated but I aspired for something more. But her bed was never cold and I often hugged pillows so she must've had something with her little theories.

One guy clearly didn't fit her stereotype and even she admitted to his being the exception to the one-dimensional man rule. Her younger brother...who I'd been madly and pointlessly infatuated with for years didn't fit the mold. When I'd be around her place he was always there...probably because he was a musician and therefore lived in her basement while he saved up to buy a house or put out a CD or whatever excuse he had to tell himself to feel ok for living rent-free in his sister's basement. Seven years younger than me, an avid pot smoker and a guy who never looked you in the eye when he spoke to you—of course I was smitten. I knew he wasn't a 'real' relationship prospect not only due to his messy rebound situation but also because he didn't seem at all interested in me in that way. I may as well have been invisible. Until one night when after more than a few beers at a party (the beer always flowed at their house –it was a constant party) we did a little smooching. Harmless enough really, yet I woke up in a blind panic, feverishly gathering my clothes like I was in some bad sitcom. I fled the scene and he mercifully pretended to sleep. I was mortified yet oddly gratified. Well--I was a grown woman after all wasn't I—we all had needs, got itches...right? No big deal. Besides it was nice to finally get the crush out of my system and I'm sure he was just feeling lonely after his breakup. So it all made sense and after a morning of berating myself and feeling humiliated, I gave an existential shrug and figured it'd never happen again. At least not until a few nights later, when I was over there again and this time there was a fire in the grate (a known aphrodisiac) and he played the guitar and sang (double whammy) yep I was a goner. So there was more smooching—clothes on this time. I left that night confused and a bit freaked out. It had been so long since I had a relationship—what was I doing? Was I avoiding building a 'real' relationship with someone more age appropriate, someone who was not, in fact, my best friend's little brother and maybe even someone who'd make eye contact once in a while? So when he started the 'fade' or the 'drift' I was both disappointed and relieved. We'd go back to being the semi-strangers we'd been for years. It would be ok. And it was. Until it wasn't. Somehow this little incident (ok two incidents) had put another blinding spotlight on an area where I felt like a complete and total failure. It had nothing to do with him specifically--I liked him and enjoyed his company, sense of humor and sweet kisses.

But let's face it, I was getting a little old for drunken hookups. So it just threw me off a bit. Then my little sister's wedding threw me off a lot more. Everything was an avalanche after that. Then suddenly it was a new year and my only resolution was not to wake up the next day...or ever. To say that seeing this friend and her brother after that was awkward was a grand understatement. I still hung out at their house but felt the flaming cheeks and throat lump of an exiled outsider. I know I overreacted and was probably making a big deal out of nothing but it became so uncomfortable over a period of several months that I started doing the 'fade' myself. The brother's walls and security system had gone up—he was sufficiently freaked out by my behavior and his imagined contributing factor (which was minimal but representative of all the previous failed interactions with men)...I think there are some things a relationship can never recover from—some friendships just don't weather the hard times as well as others. Even though we'd all weathered different challenges together, I can't help but think that when they looked at me they must've envisioned their mother's bloody cry for help and maybe they just didn't have anything left of themselves to give. I'd taken enough. Their mom's arms had eventually healed to white scars. But I still had fresh scabs over my own emotional wounds. It was a slow drift—a continental mental parting. But I got it. I think we all forgave ourselves and each other but we were tired. We needed a break from the intensity of relationships that might be callously described as dysfunctional or codependent. But those are just labels and inadequate in their judgmental undertones. I have no doubt that we'll all meet again on a new level. I bet they'll both read these sentences and shake their heads with their own valid and different interpretations. And someday maybe we'll talk about it—either over 'social' cigarettes and wine or a meal or even on the phone. Then the drift will bring us closer, tentatively at first but we'll hopefully be older and wiser then. We may just leave the words unspoken. But we'll all get the drift anyway.

Crazy is as Crazy Does

I have one friend who's been an excellent sounding board throughout my whole losing my mind and finding it again journey. Her wise advice when hearing me complain that now I felt like 'damaged goods' or like I suddenly had 'baggage' was not the pat answer – *"So what?—everybody has baggage."* Instead it was a clever approach on explaining my situation to future friends and lovers so they didn't run immediately for the door upon hearing the red flag term 'bipolar'. She said that instead of calling it an 'illness' which she knows I hate anyway, I should call it a 'condition'. Brilliant, I thought. Very inspired and a suavely subtle way to handle this delicate imagined future conversation. She says that rather than shamefully (and dishonestly) hiding my pills—I should just casually pop them before bed in front of any new boyfriend and when he asks what they're for just to say that I have this 'condition', reassure him it's nothing catching and to try and leave it at that--at least initially (she also suggested then distracting him with a lewd act that I won't mention here but feel free to let your imagination run wild on that one.) I agreed to this 'condition not illness' angle as a procrastination technique but wondered aloud how to handle it when pressed? She sighed and rolled her eyes good-naturedly reminding me that I haven't even met this fictitious person yet and wasn't I burning the uncrossed bridge just a teensy bit? But she knows I can be obsessive and wouldn't let it go until she gave me something else to work with. See—she is one of those 'matter-of-fact—doesn't give a shit what other people think of her' types. I've always envied that quality—even if it's not always the total truth it must be liberating to fake that one until you make it. I'm working on this and have made some great strides in this arena—but we still have a long way baby until I belch in public or fart in private, intimate moments. So I'm full of gas and hot air in the meantime I suppose. *And I'm ok with that.*

After some brainstorming and rejecting of ideas we sort of gave up. I was less than fond of the idea of emailing my medical records before the first date. Thought that'd be more than a little bizarre but we did have a good chuckle over that one. She said to stick to the downplaying theory under the logic that if I didn't make a big deal out of it then 'he'—my imaginary future boyfriend that is—wouldn't either. Jesus—I really was crazy wasn't I? She just shrugged and smirked saying that it never hurt to be prepared. But she did, however, draw the line at role-playing. Just as well. Once again I was getting ahead of myself and worrying over something that I currently had no control over. I have no way of knowing how someone who hasn't known me for a long time would/will respond to this potentially unsettling pronouncement. It's all well and good to say that if they freak and/or run for the hills then they were wrong for me anyway, right? And yes—there is a certain truth in that. But again—then we're in black and white territory. Could I blame someone for being scared at hearing that? No—not when considering the way that those suffering from mental 'conditions' are portrayed in films, books, on television. They are caricatures of the people I saw and stayed with during my time at the treatment facility. Yes—of course there were some of the less high functioning folks who were unfortunate enough to echo some of these grossly misrepresented images of the so-called crazy. But mostly these were the exception to the rule.

How can you tell the difference between someone with a condition and someone with a full-blown illness? That's the beauty of it—you can't. So I guess we're back to the good ol' Golden Rule then, eh? It's ironic when I think back to something my sister said during my first five-day hospitalization. She looked around at my surroundings and in a tone that I believe she meant to be comforting said... "*You're not crazy, you're just really, really sad.*" It broke my heart and I didn't know why. It was only much later I would come to understand the poignancy of that statement. Apparently this cultural idea that 'crazy' is only used to describe outwardly extreme behavior runs so deep that we don't even realize it anymore. There's not much allowance for degrees of insanity. You're either sane or you're not...and if you're not you are looked at askance and made the subject of ridicule...or worse...condescending pity. What the condescenders don't often realize in their oblivious misapplied compassion is—they are the ones who we should feel sorry for the most. Because they just don't get it and probably never will, poor dears.

Thinking outside the box

My therapist's office is up four steep slights of stairs in an old house converted into a center for social workers, psychiatrists and psychologists who all practice in a collective environment. He's in the 'penthouse' or what was once probably just below the attic if the eaves give any clue to the building's original structure. Over the last decade or so (maybe even a bit longer) I've been to about 7 shrinks and as many talk therapists (at least). In each and every one of these professionals' offices there was a distinct 'style' statement being made. Lots of African art or kitschy and charming pictures painted by children, bookshelves, certificates on the wall...something. My therapist's office is very bare. Not in a stark, cold way but in a 'this is just a temporary space and I don't need adornment--I'm here to work' sort of way. To be fair—I'd been to his private practice office before and it is a little more homey and inviting. But this place is not Zen, not minimalist, not purposely empty for Feng Shui 'flow'. It's just...bare. I used to wonder if it was subtly deliberate... as if to convey the message that we would have no external distractions on our little mind journey conversations.

The author of '*The Turning Point*', Fritjof Capra once wrote, "*Healing the universe is an inside job.*" We are all interconnected in some way but at the end of the day and upon awaking there are those moments of total aloneness. Where our thoughts reach out towards the day or night and try to bring it closer just to shut out these few disconnected nanoseconds when we drift off into a dream or pull ourselves away from one. In my therapist's office I may on the surface be discussing the events of my day or week and trying to put a framework on my thoughts, but underneath another process occurs. A quiet renewing of spirit happens through a dialogue that challenges ideas and turns them inside out. By reaching out to a skilled river guide I can navigate the rapids of my mind's meandering thoughts. He is not just a lifejacket or the expert steering a boat. He is in there with me, riding the same waves from a different perspective and we're both trying not to fall out of the boat into the rocky waters swirling around us. In this watery realm where emotion lives, he has become another more benevolent voice to add to the repertoire of self criticism that roils up threatening to engulf me and he helps me unravel these harsh thoughts and to put enough space between them. This slowing down helps me to see the black and white limitations enough to start not only to see shades of grey but glimpses of Technicolor possibilities. I sometimes play the "What if?" game...as in what if I'd met him sooner before the despair was ready to engulf me? Maybe I still would have tried to kill myself...who knows? The hindsight thing never works—it's just as bad as the apples and oranges game. Just after my attempt, my therapist talked to my dad in general terms about my situation and my dad repeated to me later a comment that puzzles me still—not because I can't recognize its truth but because I'd never really thought about it. He told my dad—"*She's so hard on herself.*" And when my dad repeated it to me it was clear that he'd never really thought about it before but that he agreed with this simple yet complex insight. In my constant barrage of inner self-flagellation, I'd become used to the ever-louder voices of self-criticism. They were in the background of every achievement always taunting "*Now what? What are you gonna do next to top this?*" I expect we're all pretty hard on ourselves to a great extent. Except for sociopaths who could certainly use a little more inner reflection if you ask me. Which you didn't—but there you have it.

What my therapist gives me, besides excellent insights and kind compassion, is an hour without the whip that I use against myself in my own mind. Nothing kinky—it's a metaphor—stay with me. It's quite a miracle to put down that whip for an hour or two a week and to experience life, even briefly, without the cringing fear of the next silent verbal beating that my mind will surely deliver. It makes me want to string these hours of freedom together and make a life worth living. To increase these hours to a day, a month, a year and so on. It is not some Pollyanna process where I go in, unload all of my 'crap' and always magically come out feeling unburdened and lighter. In a way it's similar, but it's also less dramatic and more subtle usually. It's the consistent but gentle reminders that I don't always have to be entertaining or pretty or smart or nice. It's the little reality hits that make me see that having so-called 'negative' emotions is a myth...There are no negative emotions—only negative judgments about emotions. It's the same as sanity only better—it's mental wellness. Sanity is overrated anyway. Seems boring and un-extraordinary. Anyone (or mostly anyone) can 'be sane' for moments and coast along not attracting attention to themselves or their 'quirks'. But can you be 'sane' and well? Sane and happy? I don't know. I know it takes guts to be perceived as 'crazy' and fight your way back from the darkness that can suck us all under from time to time. I know that sanity is a matter of opinion. Who is this invisible committee that made up the 'sanity' rules anyway? Did these people ever have ANY fun at all? Crazy can be fun just as it can be torturous. But it's often more the latter and therefore cancels out the former usually—at least in my own experience anyway. A lot of our conversations revolve around 'issues' that rear up for me in work environments. And I know I'm not the only one who struggles with this...

I just think if we redefined crazy in new terms it'd look something like this...

"Oh my God—wait—so you mean that you leave your house box to get in a metal car box with wheels everyday and wait in traffic with other people in their metal boxes—or sometimes you all crowd together in one metal high rise box (while listening to metal boxes with headphones) that brings you to a building with no natural sunlight or fresh air where you sit inside another cub-ick-le box, in front of a computer box for EIGHT HOURS? Then you get back in your metal box and head home, only to plop yourself in front of yet another TV box with moving pictures (after you heat up your boxed food in the microwave box) until you go to sleep on a soft bed box with metal underneath but not before setting your alarm box to wake yourself up at an ungodly hour to start this whole BOXING your way through life process all over again???....Um. that's kinda f-ed up."

Let's try and think outside the box here for a moment. If I don't want to participate in the bizarre yet 'normal' process outlined above then I'm...what? Crazy? Hmmmmm....guilty as charged I suppose. My therapist helps me make sense of some of this nonsense and keeps me sane—in my definition of sane. Which means giving myself a break from time to time if I want a breather from the 'box world' mentality. He helps me see when I'm turning off the Technicolor possibilities that exist in the box world, though, too. In other words—I don't have to be a rebel without a clue to make my point. Not that I'm sure he would phrase it that way at all. But turning a blind eye to the box world—or placing it in a bigger box stamped 'undesirable' is just another form of limited thinking. While I'm sure legions of disillusioned wage slaves would agree with me about the box's sharp edges and confining feeling—not too many of us really know how to do it differently yet. You have to work for a living but do you have to live for work? I don't think so.

I taught English in Tokyo for a year about ten years ago. This was a question I often posed to my higher-level Japanese students. *"Do you live to work or work to live?"* They frequently looked at me as though I had just sprouted nine heads and started singing "Somewhere Over the Rainbow" in French...naked. For them it was perceived as a trick question—if they answered one way they'd be seen as boring, one-dimensional losers, and if they answered another they'd be viewed as lazy—a capital offense in Japan where 12-16 hour work days are (or were at that time anyway) the norm. They were truly stumped by my persistence and I got the sick feeling after awhile that behind their chilly silences and polite smiles that they secretly just wished I would shove my stupid, annoying American riddle up my lazy, white ass—the 'please' and 'thanks very much' were implied of course. But with one group I was gratified—my question had finally hit home and sparked the lively debate I was looking for and was not dismissed as the ramblings of a judgmental outsider but appreciated for the genuine curiosity that lurked behind it. I had a stay-at-home mom, a school-uniformed teenager and a business suit-wearing 'salary man' in my cube—yes—we taught our lessons in cubes not actual classrooms since space is a commodity in Japan and must be utilized for every available inch—so the classes were small—two or three students at a shot. With this particular group, again I asked my question and waited a beat hopefully, thinking it probably would be another flop. But after a few minutes of silence, the salary man cleared his throat and told us all he'd been fired the week before and was feeling great shame about his situation. We were all flabbergasted—one; that he'd been fired but more so that he was telling us. I asked him if he felt comfortable sharing could he let us know what had happened? Keeping his eyes on the table the entire time he recounted how his boss had been unhappy with his performance for some time now but he'd been caring for his sick mother and was distracted at work. The teenager chimed in and asked if his boss knew the situation. Apparently the man had told his boss about his problem and been met with the lovely answer... *"We all have mothers, don't we?"* Here was an employer who clearly did not think outside the box. As the lesson progressed, the homemaker made some very comforting comments and said that her husband was a bigwig at Sony and might be able to help him out. By the end of the lesson we had him convinced that his personal life and his mother's health were far more important than *any* job. And besides—we all could see that his boss was a jerk and was not even worth a second thought. I was happy to work the question back in again toward the end of the lesson—and this time—for the first time, I was met with knowing smiles that included me for a change.

Hickory, Dickory, etc.

I sometimes think I was born into the wrong era and that this is where a lot of my offbeat-ness comes from. Because in some palpable way I am off a beat...semi-existing in the wrong time and therefore always trying to either slow down or catch up. When I think of all the things we humans, who invented the concept of 'time' do to it...kill it, waste it, make the most of it, hope it will heal all, lose track of it, split it up into measurements, pray for more of it, or fritter it away... it is astounding to think about, really. And rather headache-inducing. Take the biological clock for example. Weird concept to say the least. Measured in terms of a woman's eggs or her calcium breakdown or a man's weakening heart or prostate or other assorted ailments...it's a bizarre thought to envision each tiny baby born with a ticking time bomb inside them waiting to go off at any random given moment. As a child I felt time's fleeting power when the seasons seemed to come and go with the blink of an eye. Yet a boring class or the week before Christmas could go on interminably. In my teens, time was a background entity and I was still in that phase where you think you are immortal enough to innocently believe that time is on your side still. It wasn't until I hit my mid-twenties that time started to become a bit of a hostile enemy. And I remember one of those early turning points well. It was during a meeting my well-intentioned father had set up for me with one of his influential friends who had millions of dollars and was supposedly a patron of the arts. I was going to talk to him about my writing. It was an enlightening (and disheartening) experience.

Riding the train home after the meeting, my mind replayed the scene over and over again. Waiting 35 minutes to meet with the self-made Real Estate mogul in the plush downtown office, I shuffled through papers wondering what I was doing there. Waiting for information, advice...something, anything. Disembarking from the train I swim-walked home in a haze...After I'd explained that a screenplay I'd been on the verge of optioning was now...ahem...available again for potential producers (since the woman who was going to make the film had suddenly gone bankrupt) his response was what I thought of as typically corporate. "*Deals fall through all the time.* "

"OH MY GOD!" echoed in my head as I was gliding gracefully around seemingly strategically placed piles of dogshit. "*Try advertising*"... "*more stability*" Suddenly, the floodgates of absurdity opened...Some of his helpful gems:

"*Some of my friends are heroes...artistes--freelance writers, novelists.*"

(Slight condescension in the faux French accented "arteeste.")

I recalled the receptionist outside his office door who was recounting her drunken birthday weekend, gum-smacking loudly, acrylic nails tapping on the keyboard, hushed giggling into her space-age headset phone.

"Take any kind of foot-in-the-door job". He advised distractedly.

Receptionist: *"So then Johnny and Mike were brawling in the middle of the street...I know can you believe those assholes?"* Tap-tap, chew-chew.

In his office were the obligatory family photos. Ski-trip to Beach. All the seasons covered.

"But it's tough to make any kind of decent kind of living in that field." He pushed some papers around.

He was an A.D.H.D. nightmare...eyes darting everywhere and then, mercifully, he took a phone call.

After a brusque conversation with the person on the other end of the phone...I worked up my nerve a bit...

"How did you get your start?" I asked timidly.

MBA from Stanford...a chance meeting with the governor. Did he actually use the word 'gumption'? I imagined two men locked in a staring contest assessing each other; a kind of unspoken playground language of taunting dares—

"Are you up to it?"

More questions lobbed, followed by awkward, gaping, time-stopped silence.

I thanked him, made a mental note to kill my father, shook his hand...mine shaking so badly that the pumping motion was almost unnecessary, I left deflated and confused--a cavern of overwhelming exhaustion opening up inside me...Existential angst threatened to overwhelm. I had the telltale girly lump of disappointment forming in my throat. I didn't get picked for the team. I didn't even know what I was trying out for... Burning unshed tears stung the corners of my eyes. I reached out for a life preserver, clutching at anything to bring me back to center. He got another call and hastily, I excused myself and dashed for the door before I could dissolve into a puddle on his office floor.

Later, a friend's voice soothed me making all the right clucking hen sounds...

"Doesn't know you.."Hasn't read your work...Middle aged business guy...Don't let it get you down..."

Other phrases I'd heard over the years echoed in my head... *"We all have to grow up sometime. How will you pay your bills? You're so talented...You can do your writing thing on the side. (A career a la carte?) Follow your dream. Marry rich. Nature of networking--sometimes you win...sometimes you lose."*

On the way home, I stopped at the drugstore, bought a soda, looking under the cap...some marketing contest ploy? It said:

"Sorry...please try again."

And again and again. Who knew if I was born to be a writer or not and, in the meantime, I'd travel and gather material for stories, stretch my horizons beyond their limits, fall in love, get my heart shredded a few times and keep on persevering. I'd take day jobs and night jobs and third shift jobs. The clock would be a friend, an enemy and a neutral observer all the while. And I'd keep writing. I'd live paycheck to paycheck for years, yet I'd write. On the side. For me. For an invisible someday audience of readers that might connect with my words. I knew it wouldn't be easy. I knew it was a hard territory to break into—people made it sound like early pioneering, or bungee jumping into the cosmos with no cord and in a way it was—you had to be just as sturdy of constitution mentally and emotionally to withstand the harsh conditions. And you had to have endless reserves of hope. I kept that bottle cap. I have it still. Time will tell if all of that early 'struggle' paid off in some way. Aside from my meltdowns and hospitalizations—times when the wagon wheel just popped off and rolled away, I have *always* believed it was worth it. With each disappointment or rejection I became a little stronger (or a little weaker) depending on your viewpoint. And while it may sound hokey, more than being a survivor of a suicide attempt, I am also a survivor of other people's cynicism, which over time I had adopted as my own. This glass-half-empty syndrome and the who-do-you-think-you-are? attitudes may have pulled me under for a while but after a time investment and hard work, the kind without a paycheck, I kicked back up to the surface where dreams can live again. Every now and then a big wave comes crashing and I go spinning choking for air and getting entangled in seaweed. Or the clock ticks louder and I panic. And then I remember to try again. I may not be an 'artiste' but I can string some words together. I may not be a mogul but I can make a pretty box. I may not have millions but I have amazing friends and family members cheering me on. Reminding me to always *try again* and loving me forward in time. What else could a girl ask for? Well—who am I kidding—the millions would be nice really—but I do know I'm incredibly lucky nonetheless.

Itchy feet

When I was little, my grandmother had postcards and souvenirs from her trips all over Europe, a pair of castanets with little flamenco dancers painted on them from Spain, a miniature bronze Eiffel Tower from France, a shamrock encased in Lucite from Ireland, a tiny wooden shoe from Holland and an assortment of foreign coins that would be the envy of all the collectors on eBay. Whenever I went to her house for holidays or just a visit I remember these travel memorabilia fondly, they were the touchstones of my youth. As familiar as bike wheels spinning on asphalt or the scent of a freshly cut lawn, memories of the past can mingle together in a sensory kaleideoscope taking us out of the loop of linear time. Whether you believe in reincarnation or Darwinism, or the space time continuum most of us at one time or another have felt the tug of *deja vu*, had vivid dreams that later came true, knew who was calling before the phone even rang.

The mind's terrain has so many winding paths and loops that double back on themselves that it makes an Escher print seem like a kindergartener's drawing. We store snippets of the past in our heads like old clothes or toys collecting dust in an attic. We rewrite our own stories all the time. Sometimes we fall into bottomless pools where we swim around splashing in the colors of yesterday and before and what might've been. When we played until the streetlights came on it may have seemed normal, routine even. We had no 'real' concept that there were kids halfway around the world that played in minefields or ate stars for dinner. Or that there could be people who went their whole lives without seeing the ocean or snow. We lived a narrow and protected existence and that's why those things my grandmother kept on her shelf were so imbued with a feel of the mysterious. They spoke of other worlds, other times. Even the stamps on the postcards were exotic with their faded colors and postmarks. But it isn't always the grand adventures that matter. Sometimes pancakes on a rainy morning can be just as meaningful, especially when prepared with love.

My 'Nana' was always a woman far ahead of her time. She'd been one of seven sisters who miraculously (miraculous since it was so unlikely for the times) all went to college in the 1920s and 1930s. My great-grandfather, an Irish immigrant who arrived in this country with ten bucks in his pocket and cried because he couldn't go home, was a forward-thinking man who believed in education for women at a time when this was unpopular and highly unusual. A successful self-made businessman, he bought the girls furs and jewels and even weathered the Depression fairly well. My grandmother was red haired and lively—she loved to tell the tale of wearing nothing but a mischievous smile one summer at the family beach house while doing a racy burlesque dance number using the towel as a boa. In her twenties she became a chemist for Harvard Medical and worked in the labs there for 25 years. After about ten years at Harvard, my grandmother went to see the Dean of Students, a crusty old man as she described him, to ask if she could be admitted as a student. Apparently, he basically laughed at her and told her to go to Radcliff since Harvard did not 'accept women dear'. She pulled herself up to all of her 5 ft 2 inches, squared her shoulders and looked him dead in the eye saying *"Well maybe not in your lifetime sir, but definitely in mine!"* Obviously she was right but by the time it finally happened it was too late and she had a full time job and three kids to raise.

As far as I was concerned she was the most interesting, coolest, funniest and all around best-est grandmother to ever grace the planet. And I was all of that and a bag of chips to her, too. I was her *'special Courtney'* and she was *'Nana'* a word I'd come to interchange synonymously with unconditional love. There was one wry counselor at the treatment center who would roll her eyes at that phrase and say:

"Pul—eeze...you want unconditional love--get a dog!" While amusing, she'd obviously never met my Nana who oozed unconditional love from every pore. Once when I was about nine years old, my grandmother and I were going through her old photos and the international coin collection when she said that one of them was from her honeymoon promising that someday I'd have a big wedding and a honeymoon. She sighed wistfully and said she hoped she'd be around to see that day come. I asked her why she wouldn't be and she said gently that she might be in heaven by then. Wrong thing to say to a worshipful nine-year-old. I cried for three days straight and my parents were overwrought with my unrelenting sobbing until they finally managed to convince me that Nana wasn't going anywhere and that she'd be around a very long time. Skeptical and sniffling, I chose to believe them and went back to playing with my friends and forgot the whole incident. As it turned out, my high school graduation was the last milestone she was around for and again—she was right.

When she died, ironically from a cancer she'd spent the better of her life doing research on, a huge part of me went underground with her. I think that's why I viewed my death not as the end to my earthly life but as a potential reunion with the one person I'd ever really felt 'got' me on a core level. Someone who was a cheerleader for my achievements but loved me deeper and more powerfully than any A on a report card or any Spelling Bee trophy could ever add up to. Since she had gone, I thought of her (and still do) every day. She was the beacon of light in a foggy harbor and the twinkle in her eye shone more brightly than the most blazing desert sun. She was my world. She'd tickle my feet when I was falling asleep and her skilled storytelling sparked my love of travel and adventure—a different kind of itchy feet sprang up from her exotic tales of the unique customs and cultures prevailing in other countries and left no detail out when telling me all about her 14 trips around Europe. I wanted to see everything, to experience it as she had...the running of the bulls; the gondola rides in Venice, the impressive museums containing the works of all of the masters, the dusty yet awe-inspiring cathedrals and the 'fresh' boys who flirted with her. She was so glamorous and funny. She was still wearing sequins and dyeing her hair red when she was eighty. She represented everything I wanted to become. And I never got to say goodbye. I was coming home from college to see her at the hospital but I was too late, a fact I accidentally found out when I called my dad's office and his secretary started telling me where the funeral would be held. I was devastated. She was really gone and I felt like I'd never be that special to anyone again. I felt sorry for my aunts and father who'd lost their mother, for my grandfather who'd lost the love of his life and wife of fifty years. I felt sorry for the world since she was no longer in it.

Manners 101

One of the first things my grandmother taught me (besides how to spell my own name) was the basic courtesy phrases 'please' and 'thank you' rule. The emphasis was always more on the 'thank you' than the 'please' though I was instilled with the grave importance of both. There was an underlying implication that whenever you could do for yourself you needn't ask anyone else to help so 'please' was only used in dire situations. But 'thank you' were two of the most important words in the English language according to my Nana. Her rule (passed on from her mother) was that the minute you received a kindness or a gift you thanked the giver. As your fingertips touched the gift and before theirs left it. She even role played this with me—I must've been about 3 or 4 years old at the time and manners were paramount. From the moments of those early lessons on I have always been a very polite person—probably more out of habit and fear of disappointing my grandmother than true gratitude.

At the hospital, for the first time in 32 years, the pleases and thank yous virtually disappeared from my social interaction vocabulary and at first I felt guilty for not thanking the nurses for my pills or the doctors for my daily check-ins where clipboards were wielded like weaponry (or so I felt). But then it just started making sense not to say these things anymore since I didn't feel grateful and I was in a 'fuck the world' phase—so these little courtesies were the first to go (right after basic sanity and a will to live of course). I became numb to people's gifts and visits and instead of the requisite niceties I often gave an enigmatic half smile saying something like 'that's nice' and changed the subject. I simply couldn't utter these words anymore suddenly finding them both hypocritical and vapid. I was stuck in a world where words of any kind became curls of invisible smoke that wafted up and away from me just out of reach. I know a lot of people I know attributed this inattention to the ECT but that was just a convenient excuse, really. One issue I have worked on heavily over these past few years is being able to ask for what I want (something my parents would deny vehemently—it's easy to ask them and so I do). I'm referring to not only to letting go of people pleasing but to actually be able to ask people when I need help or a sympathetic ear or when I feel the crisis drumbeat echoing inside my head. This is not to say that many lovely people in my life haven't taken it upon themselves to help me, just that I am not very good at asking. But I am getting better at this skill. Admitting vulnerability and that sometimes you can't go it alone truly is a skill. Some are born with it and some are not. Some come to it later and others abuse it. Some demand loudly with entitlement and others meekly whisper while shaking. It's a worthiness issue, a style of being in the world and reflects what early messages we received about the word 'please'. Was it shown as a weakness to need and ask for help or merely a part of life that was unavoidable? Was it demonstrated as part of loving interactions that were based on two-way street relationships or was there always the taker/giver dynamic unfolding? Or maybe in some households it wasn't even a priority at all.

Slowly my pleases and thank yous came back but I was determined to try and slow down and use them in a more heartfelt manner and less as an automatic habitual response. Now when I thank the girl at the coffee shop I make sure to look her in the eye, whereas before I might've just tossed off the obligatory 'thanks' and walked away missing a golden opportunity for a real exchange. It may seem a little thing. But it can mean the world. It's important to know what you're asking for and even more important to really mean it when you say thanks.

Beyond basic courtesy or etiquette these utterances are the threads that bind us to each other. When I saw how disconnected and even downright contentious some of the client/staff relations had become on the ward it reminded me of the disconnections in my own life. It was an excellent microcosm of the ways the world at large interacts. It was hard to see beyond our roles to the person underneath. It was especially challenging for me to hold charity in my heart for the little shithead who woke us up daily with his teeth-on-edge setting voice. Mother Theresa I am not. But I digress. I did actually have a moment with the mini-dictator once. I was feeling relieved (and not a little superior) one day after I'd been discharged and gave him the 'ok' sign. He nodded in understanding as though it were akin to an apology for all the times I'd all but told him where he could stick his smarmy 'good mornings'. What I really meant in that gesture was that even though we may not have seen eye to eye (for various reasons—I was far too tall and he was far too annoying) on most things—we could still be ok with each other. Not thrilled…but ok. With some people that may just be the best you can hope for, really, and wishing for more often leads to a bloody forehead imprint on a brick wall. In my own life I'd pulled away from people just when I needed them most. It's called 'isolative' behavior and considered a bona fide symptom of various DSMIV ailments. But it's a common and natural instinct if you think about it. When an animal is hurt they separate from the pack or pride or whatever to tend to their own wounds before they rejoin the group. But the key factor is that they rejoin the group and hopefully don't just go off alone to die. For a long time I wasn't ready to rejoin the group and reveled in the safety of being around other isolators who understood this separateness syndrome. Feeling apart from things and situations and people. Feeling apart from yourself most of all.

When I said my first please to the universe (and anyone in it who would listen) during my time at the hospital it was a *'please help me stop feeling such agony'*. The second was a slightly more brazen *'please help me find my way'*. The third was the bold and daring *'please just let me feel something good about life again'*. And when each of those pleases were answered (even in the tiniest of ways) there were very loud (if internalized) *thank yous* that followed. Because then I knew that there just might be some infinitesimal point of light at the end of what had appeared to be an endlessly stretching underground tunnel. At my lowest moments I had forgotten that there was even a tunnel, let alone a light at the end.

Isn't that how so-called miracles are usually born? Quietly and sneaking up on you unexpected and unannounced? We sometimes see them as these grand dramatic gestures conveniently forgetting the fact that we planted the seeds long before they ever appeared. And then they show up in the form of a golf club and some shattered glass. Loudly and dramatically. And it's easy to overlook the hundreds of thousands of moments that proceeded that shattering. Until you go back and quite literally pick up the pieces not only of shattered glass but also of a seemingly shattered life. The real miracle for me was the removal of invisible shards from my heart and soul. It was asking for and getting the help I needed. And that's an unseen, unsung process. And it takes a really long time. Lifetimes maybe. And it also takes a hell of a lot of lipstick.

Lipstick = Love

If I could write in the sky in lipstick a message of hope to anyone reading this book it would only be this. *"Wait—it gets better"*. Not just in some pat: *"This too shall pass"* oversimplification of waiting out the pain—I think that's effective for some but not for the suicidal person. It's more of a cliffhanger sentiment--a suspense builder. And I don't want to sound like some religious nut who promises glory in the afterlife for suffering on earth. That is an equation that never added up for me. Maybe what I mean is more of a Scarlett O'Hara (one of the original lipstick girls) philosophy of life. Don't think about it now, think about it tomorrow for tomorrow really is another day. And try to truly envision a you-sized hole in the world and how tragic that would really be. Or if you prefer the George Bailey 'how my life has affected others' life review you can use that analogy. And if movie references can't even skim the surface of your despair then get help and keep getting help. And then get some more help. And write a note to God (or Goddess if you prefer)—or both to cover your bases—and to really cover your bases you can throw in Buddha, Jesus, all the saints, the Greek and Roman gods, Shiva, Allah, Fred and anyone else who might listen. Tell these beings what you need and don't be afraid to be blunt. Tell them what you want to give to the world and why you feel stymied—share with them all the things you think are getting in the way. Don't be too proud to get down on your knees if necessary. *But definitely don't stay there.*

If prayer, contemplation, talk therapy, crystals or pills haven't worked then *wait*. With the advances in technology that have happened in the last few decades who knows what the next few will bring for the mentally less well? Don't skip to the end of the book of life—it's cheating...and you rob yourself of the pleasure of letting the whole story unfold. It's cheating yourself of the beauty of the mystery of 'what if'? What if you just stuck around for awhile to see how it all turns out? What if you off yourself but were supposed to meet your soulmate the next day? What if you have a winning lottery ticket in your pocket the day you decide to jump off a bridge? What if you decide to live and I mean really, really *live*...not just survive but to thrive? What if one thing you do or say throughout the rest of your life (that you stick around to live) helps one person in some way that changes their life for the better? Think about all of the shades of the lipstick theory and apply some to your mind. There are endless possibilities and choices we can make to improve our lot in life or we can give up. Give up on ourselves, our futures, on hope, on love, on peace, on bliss. But where's the fun in that? What if you quieted the cacophony in your head and listened to the one tiny Nike voice saying "just live"?

I started to let the 'live' and 'what if' and 'wait' seeds to take root and grow over time. It took a lot of help, faith, release of pent-up rage, and good old fashioned love to get me there. Sometimes I still waver—it's to be expected. But now I have my list of questions to refer to and they really do help me, simple as it sounds. We're awfully adept at complicating simple things aren't we? God knows I've become a virtuoso at this myself. But the impatience and restlessness I've felt in the past to get to the next level as if my life were some video game is starting to ease up a bit with each passing week, month, year. I don't know what happened to my fellow journey mates who did time with me in an institution. I may never know. I just wish each and every one of them well on the remainders of their own particular paths. And I want to thank them for being in my life and showing me a multitude of things. Not the least of which is that none of us are *ever* alone even if we firmly believe that we are. I can now look at a tube of lipstick or a stretch of fabric and lace and see unborn worlds of possibility. They are not just tools of seduction or illusion or self-esteem. They are pieces to a greater puzzle and represent far, far more than glamour. And if you squint hard enough—everything has this incandescent glow of the impossible to it. It's impossible to think that we could change our lives with colored wax encased in a cylindrical plastic tube. It's inconceivable to think that a butt crack-flossing undergarment item has the ability to save our lives over and over and over again. But the love…yes…love.. that these and any items, people, and places really give off is a message we all need to hear and share. "*Stay.*" Stay long enough to care and care long enough to stay. And let these be your sword and your shield. Surrender battles but never give up on winning the war. Stop fighting yourself long enough to see the point of it all. And don't you dare leave until you do. And I promise to take my own advice on this one. Guess barring an overzealous bus or other unforeseen accidents...(sick minds don't just stop being sick—they just get ever more creative), I am here for the duration.

THE END

(well...not really)